ROMANTICS & CLASSICS

Jeremy Musson

Photography by
Hugo Rittson Thomas

ROMANTICS
& CLASSICS

Style in the English
Country House

Rizzoli
NEW YORK

New York · Paris · London · Milan

CONTENTS

page 1 A light-hearted touch: a decorative detail from an old gilt mirror finds a new home on a 1760s doorcase at Constable Burton Hall, Yorkshire.

page 2 A living still life: a corner of the Cedar Room at Smedmore, Dorset, with porcelain jars arranged on top of a marquetry cabinet on stand.

opposite The Wyvill family Labrador greets visitors in the portico of 1760s Constable Burton Hall, Yorkshire, where the family likes to sit and enjoy a view of the setting sun.

INTRODUCTION

ON STYLE

This book is a visual exploration of a selection of country houses in search of that elusive but familiar subject, English country-house style. Throughout my career I have been privileged to visit country houses all over England, particularly with *Country Life* magazine and when working with the National Trust curatorial department; with the BBC; during my heritage advisory work; and while researching and writing several of Rizzoli's beautifully produced books. As an architectural historian, my first instinct is to see country houses as artefacts that can be unpicked, understood, described and recorded. But during visits to country houses of all shapes and sizes, periods and characters, I have also come to appreciate them as part of a living culture, one that refreshes itself with every generation, forever changing in order to stay the same.

Historically, a country house was defined by its relationship to a landed estate, and that is still true for most of the houses in this book. However, the definition since the mid-twentieth century has shifted with the changing political and economic status of landowning.[1] The last hundred years were a time of particular transformation, marking the end of the centuries-old political and financial dominance, of which Mark Girouard has said: 'the mystique of land had been exploded, but the mystique of the country house remained as strong as ever'.[2] Some country houses are now preserved as historic-house museums, but even in this state they are not preserved in aspic but rather continue to develop and evolve. Within houses that remain as private homes, individual rooms may be maintained in period glory, but around these, the house and gardens continue to reshape, shift and settle.

John Goodall observed in *English House Style* (2019): 'so many of these homes accommodate a particular lifestyle associated with the outdoors – of dogs, horses, of muddy boots and riding crops. The result is that grand architecture and objects of great beauty are often mixed informally with the prosaic and the practical'.[3] Caroline

→ Looking down from the upper storey of
Beckley Park, Oxfordshire, into the dream-like
garden below.

Seebohm also noted the 'remarkable individuality' that defines the interiors of such houses; in *English Country* (1987) she described: 'a serenity to the English country interior; well-stuffed furniture, muted colours, flowers bunched heedlessly into vases, a pleasing air of informality, even in the grander drawing rooms'.[4]

This is a personal selection rather than an anthropological study, and the country houses within it are all lived in and privately owned. They include some well-known historic seats but, intentionally, a great many less familiar names and places, and both inherited houses and ones recently bought or built are featured. Taken together, they give us insight into English country life outside the house and hospitality within. The importance of colour, comfort and connection to the garden runs like a thread through all of them, albeit in different ways. Represented here are many houses, now in the hands of new generations or new owners, that illustrate the changes as well as the continuities of passing time.

English country-house style is a concept I have considered at length over the years and have come to appreciate as something that emerges from a loose ensemble of architecture, colour, furnishings and gardens. Together, these elements are framed and judged by individuals with an appreciation of history who also bring with them enjoyable strands of biography, self, family or place.

The resonance of the past includes historical influences from abroad which shows that English country houses have their own global reach. These may have arrived through trade, family connections or imperial history, or through unrestrained admiration for the visual culture of countries such as France and Italy. As Alan and Anne Gore wrote in 1991: 'The influence of the past and the influence of Continental ideas are recurrent themes in the history of English decoration'[5]; this is equally true for other cultures too, including those of India, Japan, China and the Middle East.

The twenty houses selected for this book by myself and the equally well-travelled photographer Hugo Rittson Thomas are not an attempt to reach some absolute definition of the country house or country-house style. They are a representation of the pleasure that can be shared by any interested visitor who reads the stories of the houses within these pages, enjoying the romance of what Evelyn Waugh called their 'secret landscapes'.[6]

I have grouped the houses into three important categories. 'English Romantics' looks at revived older houses, such as Haddon Hall, sixteenth-century Beckley Park, early seventeenth-century Lake House, late seventeenth-century Heale, the unforgettable early 1800s Indian-style Sezincote, and the Arts and Crafts house Vann, where architecture and garden merge most emphatically.

The 'English Classics' are fine classical examples in differing styles and scales, including the comfortable red-brick Queen Anne box at Wolverton; stately Constable Burton Hall, a handsome 1760s neo-Palladian villa; dream-like Beckside and Smedmore from the mid-eighteenth century, and Pitshill and Chyknell from the late eighteenth and early nineteenth centuries, both immaculately restored recently. There is also a new house called Eastridge, with its generous light-filled rooms that were inspired by the classical tradition and designed by Francis Terry.

The last section is devoted to the houses of the 'Artistic Eye', which belong to the creative spirits behind the gardens, interiors and ideas that shape the way we look at the country house today. Among them is Sir Roy Strong's The Laskett, with its unforgettable garden, and artist Matthew Rice's Ham Court, a fragment surviving from a fourteenth-century castle. There are visits to three homes of influential interior designers: Edward Bulmer's early 1700s Court of Noke; Draycot House, the country retreat of Emily Todhunter; and North Farm, owned by Rita Konig and her writer husband Philip Eade. At the Arts and Crafts house Voewood, like Vann, the garden blends almost seamlessly with its novel interior. Alongside these is Walcot, the sixteenth- and seventeenth-century Cotswolds home of photographer Hugo Rittson Thomas and his art consultant wife Silka, adding its contemporary twist to the country-house story.

In every house, architecture, garden and interior design play essential but different roles. The period of the building, the setting and principal materials define the character of the architecture, but these elements are also enhanced and improved by the passing of time. The evolved houses, from the stone castellated courtyard house of Haddon, to the manorial stone-and-flint Lake House and early classical red-brick Heale, are a familiar part of the English story. The enticing and gracious formality of classical houses in stone, brick or render is softened by the English landscape, while the individuality of Arts and Crafts houses, as they merge into their gardens, speaks of a different kind of design.

The interiors always intrigue. Writing in *English Houses* (2016), Ben Pentreath notes how transitory interiors can be: 'momentary … far less durable than architecture … subject to the whims of owners, of fashion, and of taste'.[7] Interior design developed its own identity as a profession in the mid-twentieth century; before that, it was in the hands of architects or professional firms of decorators and upholsterers. Key people in the mid-twentieth-century story were Virginia-born chatelaine Nancy Lancaster and the practically trained English aesthete John Fowler, who are often described as the inventors of the 'English country-house look' as it came to be understood and recognised especially during the 1970s and '80s.[8] Lancaster – with her particular Anglo-American sensibility – was mainly influential because she was a patron and socialite who knew how things worked and how important image was, and in 1948 she acquired the decorating business of Sibyl Colefax & John Fowler Ltd (Colefax and Fowler), which Fowler had first joined in 1938. Together they celebrated the charm of well-worn and aged patina, mixing elements from various periods within interiors of comfort and elegance. Cecil Beaton wrote of Lancaster that she had a talent for: 'sprucing up a stately but shabby house and making a grand house less grand. She has an adequate reverence for tradition, observes the rules of style and proportion, and manifests a healthy disregard for important furniture'.[9]

Lancaster and Fowler forged a style that worked in old houses with a wealth of attributes that just needed bringing out to create interiors of a kind of self-conscious nonchalance, suggestive of long occupation and possession.[10] In the most challenging post-war decades they gave a generation of country-house owners the confidence to make themselves at home and enjoy elegance (even without the numbers of staff around which such houses and interiors had been designed originally). In some cases, Fowler helped owners see the potential within inherited contents and encouraged them to collect carefully and appropriately for their interiors. This was at a time when the identity and purpose of these houses were undergoing dramatic change. The interiors at Sezincote include rooms that are perfect surviving examples of Fowler's approach.

But did Lancaster and Fowler really invent such a look, or was something more organic and layered going on? After all, the grouping of sofas, tables and chairs for comfortable conversation had its roots in early nineteenth-century attitudes, dubbed by John Cornforth as 'the quest for comfort'.[11] The artistic approach to interiors can also be traced to the values of the Aesthetic Movement. Country-house style drew (and still draws) on the many varieties of architecture, furniture and fabrics of differing periods – an accumulation of all that survived the ravages of taxation and sales – of the sort you might encounter in any inherited collection.

It has been fashionable among academics to regard the 'country-house look' as a fiction, a 'comfortable dream' if not a myth (or even a fraud),[12] and one that came and went. But this does not quite capture what happened, or how things look and feel today. It seems to me that a label of 'English country-house style' remains as elastic as the definition of 'the country house', and can still be applied today to houses of many different degrees of formality and finish, but it may be slightly harder to pin down than in the 1980s.

The issue of climate underscores a large part of the character of the English country house, the weather dictating the need for extra warmth for many months of the year, and perhaps a desire for colours to add brightness on grey days. This has led to very different flavours of interiors from those of the châteaux of the South of France and the villas and castles of Italy. The English country-house interior is further conditioned by the need for comfort required as a result of the traditional popularity of English country sports during the winter. For the country house, the outdoors mattered greatly; it was represented in views from the windows, in paintings, in the placing of flower or pleasure gardens close to the house and, beyond that, within the estate or surrounding countryside. It was a source of income or enjoyment, or both. In the mid-twentieth century, Vita Sackville-West talked about the country houses she admired as being those that were 'essentially part of the country, not only in the country but part of it'.[13]

English country-house gardens of the sixteenth and seventeenth centuries might have been formal, but they had a built-in expectation of domestic enjoyment. This is seen in the addition of banqueting houses in the garden or on the roof, the use of long views from the house down avenues, and the provision of opportunities to stride or ride through cultivated nature and wilderness. From the early nineteenth century onwards, country houses were designed, in effect, so that people could tumble out from them into their gardens, in search of pleasure or sport.

Although the world has altered considerably, this inside-outsideness remains a key quality of the English country house. The garden has also flowed back into the house in patterns and paintings; it persists through the chintz textiles of the eighteenth century and the revived versions of the 1980s. From the early nineteenth century, the architecture of the country house seems to have extended back out to the garden: glasshouses became flowered rooms, and outside green garden 'rooms', or enclosures, arose as places of pleasure and relaxation.

At least two generations of interior designers and decorators – not to mention gardeners and garden designers – have left their mark since John Fowler's heyday, but a view he expressed in the late 1930s still seems apposite: 'I like the decoration of a room to be well behaved but free from too many rules; to have a sense of a graciousness; to be mannered, yet casual and unselfconscious; to be comfortable, stimulating, even provocative, and finally to be nameless of period – a 'fantaisie' expressing the personality of its owner'.[14] The elusive 'fantaisie' becomes some sort of enjoyable 'réalité' in English country houses of all sizes and conditions, and country-house style continues to reside in the aesthetic and social ensemble of the house, interior and garden.

1 ENGLISH

ROMANTICS

HEALE HOUSE

The crafted art of house and garden

HEALE HOUSE, IN LUSH WILTSHIRE countryside, sits in water meadows framed by the River Avon close to the small village of Middle Woodford.[1] It appears on first sight as a mostly late seventeenth-century brick house with stone quoins, under a clay tile roof, built between 1660 and 1690. The story is in fact rather more layered than it seems initially, as the house was substantially restored and remodelled in the 1890s, by the architect Detmar Blow, and its setting further enhanced with memorable gardens on which Harold Peto advised between 1906 and 1911.[2]

House and garden together form an essay in Englishness, the late nineteenth- and early twentieth-century revival, inside and out, informed by high artistic values, and all has been gently revivified by its current owners Guy and Frances Rasch, in whose family the estate has been for more than a century. Inside, since the couple took on the house just over two decades ago, there have been a number of judicious alterations, most especially the modernising of the old kitchen and opening it up to a light-filled family sitting room.[3] The memorable aesthetic qualities of the house's interiors have also been enhanced with modern touches – including advice from designer Penny Morrison for the dining room – in the form of simple, elegant textiles and bold wallpapers, as well as subtle contemporary additions to the established gardens.[4]

The historic core of the property is the modest seventeenth-century manor house, which was probably built by a

lawyer, Sir Robert Hyde, possibly retaining part of a sixteenth-century house.[5] The original five-bay south front, with its late seventeenth-century cross-windows, is crowned with a diminutive pediment projecting into the clay tile roof. The original house was substantially extended in the late eighteenth century but reduced back to this late seventeenth-century core after a major fire in 1835. It then became a tenanted farmhouse for the next half century.[6] In 1894 the house was purchased by the Hon. Louis Greville, a younger son of the 4th Earl of Warwick who had been the second secretary of the diplomatic service in Japan. He also managed to put together a reasonably substantial landed estate around the house.

Greville employed the architect Detmar Blow to renew, as Lawrence Weaver said in 1915, 'the ancient amenities of Heale' – although in truth many of the amenities were entirely new.[7] Blow extended the accommodation of the house and remodelled the interior. In the fashion of a number of Blow's artistically minded patrons at the time, Greville wanted to make the mellow older house into a new one, but for the considerable additions to be designed in just the same spirit as the older house.

As Gervase Jackson-Stops wrote in 1986, 'the boundaries between restoration and inventions were blurred' in much of Blow's work on these houses.[8] Late eighteenth-century sash windows were replaced with new stone mullions and

↑ An unforgettable harmony was created by Detmar Blow's admirable 1890s restoration of the late seventeenth-century brick house, which included the new range in a similar style to the right.

→ This Japanese teahouse was built by four Japanese artisans who were brought to England especially for the purpose. The gardens were designed between 1906 and 1911 with advice from Harold Peto.

← Heale House's elegant drawing room, designed by Detmar Blow in early eighteenth-century style, with its comfortable modern sofas and cushions covered in fabrics from India and the Middle East.

→ The drawing room is centred on views of the garden with woodland framed beyond.

transomed cross-windows, the original style of fenestration.

Blow was an idealistic figure, much influenced in his early years by his friendship with John Ruskin and William Morris, and who worked with Philip Webb at Clouds House in Wiltshire. Blow designed Wilsford Manor, also in Wiltshire, in flint and stone, honouring the traditional palette of historic buildings in the region. He was the favoured architect of the leading intellectual figures and artistically minded aristocrats known as 'The Souls', and then became the architect to the Mayfair estate of the 2nd Duke of Westminster.[9]

At Heale, Blow took a bold but artistic approach to reviving the house. He enlarged it significantly to the south-west (creating a new front of nine bays) by repeating the south-west elevation of the original house in an almost mirror image. He added a substantial range to the south-east, which was stepped back. This provided one huge drawing room, facing the garden, and the entrance hall to the north-west – the latter part self-consciously on the foundations of a lost range. He also added a kitchen pavilion in a diminutive version of the original house to the north side. This is a process so different from modern approaches to extending old buildings that it takes a while to appreciate the sheer fun and artistry of it all.

Blow created a substantial new entrance hall to the north-west in the manner of an early seventeenth-century great hall, panelled and given a Jacobean-style plasterwork ceiling. This leads through to a splendid late seventeenth-century staircase brought from another house and of a considerably larger scale and more dramatic than would have been found there originally. Above the staircase, an eighteenth-century ceiling painting of *Venus and Mercury* rescued from a London house was inserted to add to the baroque effect.

Blow's triumphant addition in terms of the interior was the huge drawing room, with an essentially neo-Palladian character enhanced by a coffered plasterwork internal dome also apparently rescued from a London house then being demolished. While this feels very connected to the gardens, it should not be underestimated how, in the 1890s/early 1900s era, the house was being contrived to be a setting for a collection of furniture and paintings, reflecting the Aesthetic Movement taste of Greville and his wife, Lily.

In 1906–11 the Grevilles developed remarkable gardens at Heale with Harold Peto, who had been the architectural partner of Sir Ernest George. Peto's own home was Iford Manor with its famous terraced gardens. The gardens at Heale were partly formal and Renaissance-inspired around the house, framed with stone paths and terraces, yew hedges and lawn. Peto also helped oversee the Japanese-inspired elements, which were especially important to Greville, as he had spent time there in the diplomatic service.

A thatched timber-frame teahouse was built by four Japanese craftsmen who came to England specially for the purpose; the vivid red-painted Japanese bridge is a scaled-down copy of the famous sacred Nikko Bridge that leads to a garden of shrines and temples (also known as the Shinkyo Bridge). Peto himself had also visited Japan in 1898, and had already designed a Japanese garden for Easton Lodge, Essex, in 1902, for

↑ The master bedroom walls are hung with an attractive pink toile de Jouy pattern on a pale yellow ground.

↑ The principal staircase was created in the 1890s from a late seventeenth-century original bought in from another house.

→ Modern comforts: a recently
created living room, which opens
directly to the family kitchen.

Greville's sister-in-law, Daisy, Countess of Warwick (with pergola, water garden and Japanese teahouse).

While the estate remained in family hands throughout the twentieth century, for a brief period after the Second World War Heale House was in institutional use, but in 1959 became the home of Major David Rasch, Louis Greville's great-nephew (Greville's only son having died in the First World War), and his wife, Lady Anne Somerset, sister of the 11th Duke of Beaufort.

In 1968 the Rasches reordered the house, removing one of the bays on the entrance front to bring more light to that side of the house, and resiting Blow's baroque front door. They also removed the plaster dome of the drawing room, dividing the double-height drawing room horizontally to add more bedrooms to the house. Lady Anne took a special interest in reviving the Edwardian gardens and created the tunnels of espaliered apple trees in the former kitchen garden with its ancient textured walls.

Heale House is now the home of the next generation of the family, Guy and Frances Rasch and their two children. Frances Rasch is a professional garden designer and has continued to 'evolve and simplify' the garden. She has given the areas that merge with meadows around the house special attention, to provide year-round colour, including swathes of bulbs, a collection of magnolias and wildflower planting. New borders have been created to 'add contemporary drama' to the garden.

Frances Rasch is very conscious of working on a garden on which other family members have worked: 'Everybody gardens in a different way and plants react to gardens in different ways. Managing a garden like this in the twenty-first century is very different to the way Louis Greville managed with nine gardeners. The composition of the house, its setting and the garden framework laid out by Harold Peto have a very timeless feel. The work of my mother-in-law's and ours is layered on top – it all adds to an organic growth, but somehow always retains the same spirit that I first saw'.[10]

Inside the house, Frances Rasch has gently modernised and lightened some of the rooms, making them more comfortable. The inner hall (an anteroom to the dining room) is hung with a Bernard Thorp fabric with a chintz-inspired pattern, and crowded with the hats and coats that always speak of a country life. The main staircase hall landing, with its rich detail, panelling and painted ceiling, has a bold Neisha Crosland coral pink and aubergine wallpaper, which works especially well with the family portraits on the surrounding walls. Bedrooms are light and comfortable, the bedroom corridor painted pale blue and white, the master bedroom walls hung with an attractive pale yellow-ground and pink toile de Jouy, and the main guest bedroom hung with an antique floral fabric and a Noblesse Fontaine wallpaper, with curtains from Ian Mankin.[11]

The main south-facing drawing room was redecorated in a suitably Edwardian pale green – courtesy of the 1996 film of Henry James's *The Portrait of a Lady* (1881). James's opening description of the house has something of the flavour of Heale: 'a long gabled front of red brick, with the complexion of which time and the weather had played all sorts of picturesque tricks, only, however, to improve and refine it'.[12]

→ A window at Haddon Hall, Derbyshire, looking out onto the famous terraced gardens of the house, which were first laid out in the sixteenth century.

HADDON HALL
A family with history

HADDON HALL IS A DREAM OF A house: the essence of Englishness. It is formed by two courtyards laid onto a hillside, with terraced gardens surrounded by woodlands, on a spur of the River Wye. The greenness of its site enhances the earthy palette of the building's Derbyshire gritstone and limestone. Haddon Hall is the epitome of the ancient house that has grown over the centuries: it is a layered accumulation of building dates, and substantial sections of the outer walls are from the late twelfth century.[1]

The Great Hall (known as the Banqueting Hall), great chamber and ancient and atmospheric kitchens, which form the central range (with an upper and a lower courtyard to either side), belong to the fourteenth century. The domestic Chapel on the south-east corner, which

also serves as a parish church, has one of the finest surviving historic interiors in Derbyshire, with its early fifteenth-century decorative wall paintings, and early seventeenth-century family pews and monuments; it is mostly from the thirteenth and fifteenth centuries. The four-storey entrance tower was completed in around 1530, while the Long Gallery – known in the twentieth century as the Ballroom – was formed (principally) in the late sixteenth century. The garden terraces were laid out at the same time.

No designer could have envisioned the effect of the composition on modern visitors, many of whom quite naturally assume they are looking at a castle, but it is more accurately described as a fortified manor house; crenellations were, in the later medieval period, as much a sign of

← ← Haddon Hall, seen at a distance, appears like a castle in a fairy tale, a house of timeless and mellow beauty.

↓ The house took its current form in the sixteenth century, and has changed little since that time. It was lovingly restored by Lord Edward Manners's grandfather, the 9th Duke of Rutland. This view shows the central hall and chamber range.

→ The colour of the stone and light reflected from ancient glass are all part of the appealing aesthetic of this remarkable house.

status as of defence. The house is today the home of Lord Edward Manners and his wife Gabrielle (Lady Edward Manners) and their young family. Lord Edward is the youngest son of the 10th Duke of Rutland, and when his brother David inherited the principal estate at Belvoir Castle in Leicestershire, he inherited the estate at Haddon Hall.

Haddon Hall was originally built by the Vernon family and came to the Manners family in the 1560s, through a marriage of one Sir John Manners to Dorothy Vernon. When their grandson became the 1st Duke of Rutland, Haddon Hall, after 1700, became a secondary house to Belvoir Castle, and, despite being the centre of a large landed estate, was in truth a barely occupied property throughout the eighteenth and nineteenth centuries: part of

it was occupied by servants who looked after it, with occasional events taking place there.

The sense of history at Haddon Hall is extraordinary. The Parlour has an important Tudor painted ceiling of Tudor roses and heraldic panelling. The 33-metre Long Gallery was designed by leading Elizabethan proto-architect Robert Smythson. In the 1920s, however, it became a major restoration project of Lord Edward's grandfather, the 9th Duke, who had set himself the task of making the house sound and comfortable, while preserving the remarkable aesthetic much admired by visitors. Novelist Henry James, for instance, who visited in the 1870s, approved of 'the silent courts and chambers, with their hues of ashen grey and faded browns', but regarded it as

something akin to the haunting ruins of Pompeii as evidence of a vanished civilisation almost frozen in time.[2]

The 9th Duke, then Lord Granby, was probably influenced by his artist mother Violet, who had already restored the tapestries and collected oak furniture for the house and who treated the old house itself as a work of art, to coax it back to life. He turned it into a proper family home, adapting the ancient buildings. He used local workmen, managed by a clerk of works, Leonard Stanhope, and mason, William Barker of Bakewell, while the joiner Fred Smith, in 1923–24, brilliantly recreated a fifteenth-century roof for the Banqueting Hall (using the drawings by Sir Harold Brakspear and timbers cut from the estate), which had been replaced in around 1800.[3] He became a friend of Howard Carter and, as Michael Hall has observed: 'It was the Duke's ability to banish the atmosphere of decay without losing the patina of age which is so impressive today'; so much depended on 'his sensitive eye, romantic imagination and archaeological discipline'.[4]

This atmosphere can be experienced in the two courts and the Banqueting Hall, where the timber roof was exactingly repaired and recreated, and the Long Gallery, where the Duke insisted on the greatest care being taken to preserve the ancient appearance of the glazing pattern

←← The sixteenth-century Long Gallery is a room where the family would stroll and talk in wet weather, or enjoy the views over the terraced garden. These were prestige chambers that could be used for multiple purposes.

↑ Lord Edward and his wife Gabrielle (Lady Edward) have brought contemporary touches and furnishings to several of the ancient rooms of Haddon Hall.

↓ The atmospheric Banqueting Hall, or Great Hall, as restored by the 9th Duke.

→→ The family drawing room. No curtains, just simple new-oak shutters; the walls are painted in a dark blue-grey, often used in art galleries, from Edward Bulmer's paint line.

and the faded browns of the panelling. He celebrated the completion of the restoration by commissioning Rex Whistler to paint a panel to go over the fireplace to replace a damaged original. The painting captures perfectly the idealised, almost ethereal quality of the house in its setting. Like an illustration from an illuminated manuscript such as the fifteenth-century *Les Très Riches Heures du Duc de Berry*, the Duke and his young son and heir gaze wistfully in a kind of reverence.[5]

In the Chapel, the Duke commissioned Professor Tristram, who helped restore the early fifteenth-century wall paintings illustrating the lives of St Nicholas and St Anne. The south wall features a particularly delicate treatment of interwoven lines of plants, leaves and flowers, originally bright but now faded, having once been covered with whitewash (under which the painting was spotted by the Duke's eight-year-old daughter, Lady Ursula d'Abo).[6] There are also surviving examples of fifteenth-century stained glass, and the 9th Duke acquired the remarkable alabaster reredos in 1933, installing it himself in a wooden frame.

Lord and Lady Edward Manners moved into the house in September 2018 and occupy the family apartments in the north and the east corner of the upper courtyard, including the Peverel Tower, the Duke's Tower and the rooms that had formed the nursery wing in the 1920s adaptation. They had previously been

living in the Bowling Green pavilion, as Gabrielle, Lady Edward Manners, recalls: 'a lovely building just up the hill, with its own terraced garden, which Edward had done up in 2002. We moved in initially just for a weekend, and then did not go back. We waited and we watched the house for a year and thought about how it worked before doing anything. At first it was pretty cold but good fires helped. Then to make it warmer, I put in two layers of curtains over the windows, and also added curtains to the stairwells. The house is mostly only one room deep, all laid out in a figure of eight. The spaces are wonderful and beautiful – shockingly beautiful'.[7]

'We are very grateful to the 9th Duke who put in good plumbing in the 1920s, and brought in so much good early English furniture, which looks wonderful in this setting. I collect modern art and wanted to make some connections between the modern and the old. We found great chests of yellow silk curtains and we have brought many out and used them – we found Sibyl Colefax's name in the 9th Duke's visitors' book and wonder if she advised. We keep finding things'.

Colours have been important to the establishment of a new home at Haddon Hall, including a dark colour in the drawing room: 'Pale colours just didn't work with the plaster walls, simple oak shutters to the windows and open fireplaces, so we chose a dark retiring colour, similar to that used in art galleries. It's a Bulmer colour, a dark blue-grey'.

Lord and Lady Edward Manners have created a new dining room in the tower:

↑ The new dining room in the former Great Chamber of the Eagle Tower, decorated by Lord and Lady Edward Manners, and lit only by candles and firelight at night.

the original Great Chamber in the Eagle Tower, which had become a furniture store – 'it took a whole month to clear this room, with its wonderful Tudor fireplace, and we only light it with candles at night. Haddon surprises you constantly and bringing the house to life is really good fun. We are very conscious of the history of former inhabitants. The 9th Duke kept a detailed journal and we often feel we are following quite closely in his footsteps.'

The terraced gardens, much admired for their sense of structure and connection to the house, step down towards the River Wye, providing vistas of the parkland and Peak District beyond. They were first laid out by Smythson when he was working on the Long Gallery, creating a Renaissance stone framework of levels, staircases and balustrading, all intended to enhance the view from the Gallery. The climbing roses and clematis and formal fountain were added by Kathleen Manners, the Duchess of Rutland, who supported her husband's 1920s restoration.

From 2008 Arne Maynard, the award-winning garden designer, has been developing the gardens 'not to slavishly recreate something Elizabethan, but to recapture the spirit of the Hall, with its wonderful mix of history and palpable sense of romance'.[8] This spirit is achieved by balancing different elements: 'on the fountain terrace roses and mixed herbaceous [plants] create full and romantic borders against the terrace walls; whilst wildflower meadows embroidered with martagon lilies and orchids, and rare species tulips, create a soft transition into the landscape beyond'. New hornbeam and beech topiary have also been planted to complement the layered quality of the building itself. The garden is another meeting point of the old and the new.

BECKLEY PARK

A spiritual retreat in brick

SOME OLD COUNTRY HOUSES SEEM
to be suspended in a particular atmosphere, a feeling that emanates from the
mellow beauty of their materials, while
gardens and nature weave further layers around them. The English ideal of
the artistic unity of building, garden and
landscape is nowhere more vivid than at
Beckley Park, where the compactness and
simplicity of the architecture create their
own magic. Although it is only a few miles
from Oxford, Beckley retains a special
aura of remoteness and ancient history
that clings to this moated Tudor residence,
now the family home of Amanda Feilding,
Countess of Wemyss and March. James
Lees-Milne, visiting in August 1972, wrote
that it was 'A most romantic, timeless old
house like the end of a delicious dream, a
harbour one longs to go to'.[1]

Beckley is indeed an ancient place.
The original castle (of 'Beccaule') on
the site is thought to have been built by
Alfred the Great in the ninth century as
a motte and bailey with one moat, and
was bequeathed to a kinsman, Osferth.
After the Norman Conquest of 1066, it
became the capital seat of the Honour
of St Valery.[2] The estate was granted
by Henry III to his brother, the Earl of
Cornwall, in 1227. During the thirteenth
and fourteenth centuries, the site was a
hunting lodge for the royal family, with
buildings including a hall, chambers,
chapel, kitchen and stables; a garden and
vineyard were also recorded.[3] The lodge
was rebuilt for Edward III from 1373, the
period from which the present triple moat
complex – which adds so much to the
character of Beckley Park – is thought

←← A sculpted form in rosy brick: Beckley Park was built around 1550 as a hunting lodge, and is famous for its gabled turrets; the central one is a staircase, and to either side the turrets were garderobes, or latrines with chutes into the moat, which, in the sixteenth century, were state of the art for heavy-drinking hunting parties.

↓ The entrance of Beckley Park: originally there was also a three-storey central porch, similar to the three towers at the back of the house. The diapered brick patterning marks this out as a building of some status.

to date. The hunting lodge is assumed to have been ruinous by the mid-sixteenth century when it was acquired in c. 1550 by Sir John Williams (later Lord Williams of Thame) and it most likely was then entirely replaced with the building that stands on the site today. Lord Williams also acquired and rebuilt a great country house at Rycote around this time, of which only a part remains.[4]

The five-bay red-brick entrance front of Beckley Park is handsomely diapered, its original two-storey front tower having fallen down and been replaced at some point by a single-storey porch. Windows are stone mullion and transom, with a neat drip mould. The face to the inner moat has three narrow, three-storey gables that rise precipitously to small gables no bigger than dormers. Mark

Girouard has argued that this last feature appears to reflect the hunting lodge status of the building, with the first-floor lodgings generously supplied with two garderobes (or latrine closets): one in the west and one in the east. These were the up-to-date thing for heavy-drinking hunting parties, and are placed at either side of a staircase turret with handsome timber treads.[5]

Christopher Hussey wrote in *Country Life*, in 1929, that these gables 'constitute the architectural beauty of the house'.[6] However, the interiors provide their own matchless aesthetic quality, with mellow aged oak and pale-ochre colour-washed walls and old panelling, complemented by English and Italian tapestries and antique furniture.

The compact central hall has a broad fireplace, and to the west lies the panelled

→ Beckley Park seen from the inner of the three moats, which were part of the original medieval construction.

↓ The intimate and stately yet modestly sized hall of Beckley Park forms a handsome drawing room with its large hearth and comfortable low sofas; its atmosphere is lovingly protected by Amanda Feilding, Countess of Wemyss and March.

parlour; to the east, the buttery and old kitchen. The latter, with its broad hearth, became a dining room in the early twentieth century and the whole house still carries the dreamy air of an aesthetic restoration carried out in the early 1920s, a project overseen by Lady Wemyss's grandparents, Percy Feilding and Clotilde Brewster. The restoration of Beckley Park was managed by Clotilde, a task for which she received little recognition until a recent study by American scholar Laura Fitzmaurice.[7]

Clotilde Brewster was a Henry-Jamesian American brought up in Florence, Italy, and France among poets and artists. She was the daughter of the philosopher Henry Brewster and his aristocratic German wife, Julia von Stockhausen, who restored the château d'Avignonet, near Grenoble, before it was destroyed by fire in 1882. Clotilde was an extraordinary figure, 'one of the first women to professionally practice architecture internationally'.[8] At the age of eighteen, in 1893, she was one of five women to exhibit designs in the Women's Building at the World's Columbian Exposition (or World's Fair) in Chicago. She was among the first women to study mathematics at Cambridge University before being apprenticed in the office of architect and garden designer Reginald Blomfield.[9] She also designed the Renaissance Revival–style Palazzo Soderini, overlooking the Piazza del Popolo in Rome, when she was only eighteen years of age. Percy Feilding and Clotilde met while they were both training

with Blomfield and married in 1904. One of their first joint commissions was for the Hon. Terence Bourke, to restore and add a new wing to Pekes Manor in Sussex.

For themselves, they acquired Stonehill, a run-down house in Sussex, in 1911. This was, in many ways, the precursor to their project at Beckley, and good preparation for the art of living simply for the sake of their artistic ideals. A visiting friend, Logan Pearsall Smith, wrote: 'They live in an ancient and picturesque cottage, or small farm-house, in discomfort which is almost squalor'.[10]

From 1920 onwards, their project was Beckley Park, which had, for some years, been a modest tenant farmhouse. They adapted it with discretion, echoing the style and values of the Aesthetic Movement. Hussey noted the 'admirable

↑ The atmospheric oak-panelled parlour beyond the hall, with its Tudor fireplace, is hung with faded gold-coloured Italian brocades.

↑ The dining room, formed out of the mid-
sixteenth-century kitchen during a 1920s restoration,
with its fitted sideboard filled with antique plates.

→ Beckley Park's garden rooms and enclosures are
places of resort, conversation and entertainment, all
within a moated frame.

judgment of the Feildings' in *Country
Life*,[11] especially praising the appropriateness of mellow Italian furniture in
this English Renaissance house. A letter
written in 1920 by Clotilde to her brother
celebrates the acquisition of Beckley
Park, noting 'the house is famous. Sir
Alfred Mond wanted to buy it. Asquith
went there the day after we bought it'.[12]

The artistic compositions of old
furnishings and textiles were – and are –
important to Beckley, as they had been
to Stonehill. Clotilde wrote to her brother
of the latter: 'We have brought the carved
cassone into the entrance and hung
Arthur's red brocatelle over it. It looks
stunning with the gilt looking glass you
gave me hanging over it. You would not
recognize the house. It looks elegant and
theatrical, no longer humble and sordid'.[13]

The yew topiary and knot garden were
laid out by the Feildings from 1920, to
the north and east of the house. Creating
a pleasing organic picture when viewed
from the house, these are a romantic
dream of a space where figures, forms
and shapes loom over the narrow lawns
like characters in a play; tightly packed
within box and yew hedges, they are
exaggerated in an almost baroque
spirit, yet also somehow very subtle and
very English.

The Feildings were part of the Oxford-
Bloomsbury circle, and Philip and Lady
Ottoline Morrell helped them find the
house.[14] Aldous Huxley was a regular visitor, walking over the fields from Oxford
and famously taking inspiration from the
house for the fictional manor Crome in his
audacious novel *Crome Yellow* (1921).

The house party described in its pages
is modelled on Philip and Lady Ottoline
Morrell's Garsington Manor (also close

to Oxford), but there can be no doubt the
house itself is inspired by Beckley Park:
'They had descended … the steep yew-
walk that went down, under the flank of
the terrace, to the pool. The house tow-
ered above them, immensely tall, with the
whole height of the built-up terrace added
to its own seventy feet of brick façade,
enhancing the impression of height'. The
character Henry Wimbush delivers an
amusing lecture on the imaginary builder
of the house, Sir Ferdinando Lapith,
the supposed author of 'Certaine Priuy
Counsels by One of Her Maiestie's Most
Honourable Priuy Counsel, F.L. Knight'
in which the matter of 'the proper placing
of his privies' was dealt with 'with great
learning and elegance'.[15]

Despite the obvious romance of it all,
the house was bitterly cold in winter, as
illustrated by a letter written by Percy to
Clotilde's brother, describing how they
had taken refuge in the kitchen. 'C. is
cooking the supper & S. is engaged in
a work of art. I am sitting writing on my
knees, clad in a fur coat bought at Munich
& with my feet in the oven: the hot plate
is my table; the odour of pork sausages
frying within a yard of me.'[16]

Amanda Feilding recalls a rather
Spartan, if romantic, isolated childhood,
when there was no money for heating and
the house had no hot water, but a lot of
'interesting conversation and debate'.[17]
At the age of sixteen, she left her convent
school and set out to see her Buddhist
monk godfather Ñāṇamoli Bhikkhu, in
Ceylon, who was her father's closest
friend, formerly Osbert Moore, and an
author who translated from Pali the semi-
nal Buddhist text *The Path of Purification*
(1982). Amanda never made it to Ceylon,
having been waylaid in Syria, where

she lived with the Bedouin. A devoted custodian of Beckley Park, she set up the Beckley Foundation in 1998 and has since carried out pioneering scientific research into consciousness and its changing states, and into the therapeutic value of the psychedelics. Amanda has been called the 'hidden hand behind the psychedelic renaissance' and her work has helped reform global drug policy.

James Lees-Milne remembered the Basil Feildings as being 'dedicated to the place as to a delicate and precious child'.[18] Under the care of Amanda Feilding, Beckley Park has been made more comfortable but still retains its artistic air, which has been enhanced by other careful touches. To the faded fabrics and Italian furniture have been added textiles from India and the Near East, paintings by Amanda and also by her father Basil Feilding, an accomplished artist who rarely exhibited. She describes him as very anti-establishment: 'charming and diffident, he was devoted to beauty' and to Beckley.

↑ The bedroom at the very top of the house has a sloped ceiling and walls lined with bookcases.

→ The Captain's Room ceiling, copied from a historic example and installed in Lake House, Wiltshire, during a 1990s restoration.

LAKE HOUSE
The revival of atmosphere

LAKE HOUSE – ONCE ALSO KNOWN as the Manor of Lake – was built near Wilsford in Wiltshire, in 1578, for George Duke, a wealthy cloth merchant from Devon. The word Lake does not, surprisingly, refer to a lake, but derives from the Saxon word for running water. Previously the site was occupied by a house belonging to John Capelyn, and this earlier building was either absorbed into – or entirely replaced by – the late Elizabethan Lake House. The property then passed through George Duke's descendants for nine generations, until 1897.[1]

Its exterior of chequerboard knapped flint and local Chilmark limestone – the same stone used for nearby Salisbury Cathedral – creates a rooted, textured appearance as Lake House rises up from the surrounding hillside. The south-west entrance side has five gabled bays, with double-height canted and crenellated windows and a dramatically tall, two-storey crenellated porch with a round-arched door, all of which emphasise the castle-like impression of the building. Christopher Hussey rightly regarded this house as a 'late Gothic masterpiece' defined by 'renaissance symmetry' and a 'gem on Avon's silver ribbon'.[2] It is often compared to nearby Stockton House, but there the flint is used in bands, compared to the chequer treatment at Lake House.

A 1752 estate plan shows the house surrounded by formal gardens with three avenues of trees extending from the south-west. The house was enlarged at some point in the eighteenth century, although nothing of this is now visible apart from the handsome stone gate

piers on the road. In 1838, while in the ownership of renowned antiquary Reverend Edward Duke, the house was severely damaged by fire, but was restored to its historic character rather than being rebuilt in a new style or fashion.[3] After Duke's widow sold the house to Joseph Lovibond in 1897, it was further restored by the Arts and Crafts architect Detmar Blow with advice from Philip Webb and the Society for the Protection of Ancient Buildings (SPAB).

Still handsome and venerable-looking, it comes as a surprise to learn that Lake House suffered a second significant fire in 1912; this was even more devastating than the first and was followed by major restoration and extension. Blow was again appointed, this time by tenant Percy Illingworth, and the essentially L-shaped ground plan dates from this early twentieth-century rebuilding. It included alterations and extensions to the north, east and south-west, and the north side of the house gained a

single-storey stable wing of rendered brick, which curves around a service yard.

Colonel Bailey, a director of the Wilton Carpet Company, later leased and then bought Lake House from the Glenconner family, living there with his wife Lady Janet Bailey, daughter of the 1st Earl of Inchcape. They appointed Darcy Braddell to make further alterations in 1922. Braddell was a Scottish architect who had been articled to Sir Ernest George before carving out a career working on country houses in a well-informed Arts and Crafts spirit. This included work at Melchet Court in Hampshire, in 1914, for industrialist Sir Alfred Mond, later Lord Melchett; Braddell also adapted Mond's house in Smith Square, London. It was Braddell who added the handsome barrel-vaulted dining hall to the south-east corner of the house, with a huge mullioned and transomed oriel window looking towards the river; the fine plasterwork ceiling of the dining room, modelled on that of the Great Chamber of South Wraxall Manor

↑ The highly distinctive texture and pattern of the façade of Lake House is created by flush flint panels alternating with local stone.

←← The Captain's Room has a modern painted frieze that was commissioned by Sting and Trudie Styler on the advice of Alain Mertens. It was inspired by historic examples and based on a design by Mertens.

in Wiltshire. Together with additional domestic offices on the north-east corner, this forms a well-judged, stepped composition. The Bailey family lived at Lake House until 1991.

The house remains in wonderful condition. Its tall, stone-built profile set on a hillside – with gabled stone and flint looking out over gentle water meadows – continues to represent an English ideal. Its interiors are artistic yet comfortable, the gardens planted and shaped to enhance the surrounding landscape. It is now the home of the musician Sting (Gordon Sumner) – formerly lead singer, bassist and songwriter for The Police, and a solo artist since 1985 – and his wife, actor and film producer Trudie Styler. As well as providing a family home for the couple and their four children, Lake House has been a place of music-making, and the setting for work on films, albums and other projects. Sting composed all the songs on his album *Ten Summoner's Tales* here, including 'Fields of Gold', directly inspired by Lake House's landscape setting amid fields and wildflower meadows.[4]

Ms Styler recalls: 'On that clear, cold day when I first saw Lake House, I was captivated by the romance of it all'. The couple found 'the spirit of the house was warm and welcoming, its history positive and life-affirming',[5] and, after buying it in 1991, they spent five years restoring and updating the fabric, making the interiors work for a modern family while preserving the charming qualities that drew them to the house in the first place. The gardens have been revived and refashioned in a romantic sprit, with advice from Arabella Lennox-Boyd, and new kitchen gardens created. Ms Styler recollects in the foreword to her book devoted to cooking with

organic vegetables raised in their own kitchen garden: 'Moving to Lake House brought back to me my childhood dream of living on a farm'.[6]

The restoration project was managed with advice from their friend, the versatile Belgian-born interior designer Alain Mertens, who studied at Columbia University and in Vicenza and worked extensively in Europe, including on the creation of suites for the Hotel George V in Paris. Mertens (who died in 2017) was based in New York and had advised on the couple's New York apartment; in his role at Lake House, he was responsible for the overall feel of the decoration and furnishing of the house, using an approach that he described as one of 'eclectic classicism, that includes modern'.[7] He stressed the importance of respecting the history of Lake House. Ms Styler has also celebrated 'the vision and expertise of many craftspeople', such as the thirty-five-strong team of dedicated builders, headed by Roger Davies, who helped them reach into the heart of Lake House and 'bring out its atmosphere'. She recalls that 'when they finally left it seemed quite empty'.[8]

The main entrance hall of Lake House runs between two parlours – originally a dining parlour and a common parlour – leading to an eighteenth-century staircase hall now open to the central family living room beyond. The living-room walls are covered in a bold damask-pattern paper and hung with Italian Old Master paintings on panel, and a new plasterwork ceiling has been added to complete the effect. An old leather sofa faces the sixteenth-century hooded chimneypiece, and there are velvet-covered sofas with tapestry-fragment cushions. Everywhere

→ A framed view: the stately oriel window in the main dining room, added in the 1920s, gives a fine view of the river below.

there is an abundance of texture and the feeling of comfort that belongs to a well-loved family home. Fabrics feature heavily in the Map Room, which is hung in a striped textile with a tartan carpet and hunting-lodge-style chairs formed from antlers.[9] Ms Styler has said of the interiors that 'wherever possible we have used fabrics on the walls, rather than paper, particularly in the bedrooms'.

Copies of early seventeenth-century plaster ceilings were introduced into the Music Room and Captain's Room – the latter dominated by a huge crafted model of a two-masted brig – on the south side of the house. The bold friezes around these rooms were painted to a design by Mertens to reflect the period, with animals darting in and out of the trees in a stylised landscape. The frieze in the central lobby has figures in sixteenth-century dress playing musical instruments and singing, and in the master bedroom there are painted imaginary figures who seem to have escaped from a masque. Fittingly, there are musical instruments throughout the house, with those in the Music Room including lutes, flutes and a spinet that once belonged to the diarist Samuel Pepys.

The stately 1920s dining hall, fitted with historic early seventeenth-century panelling, was for a time used as a recording studio, but has reverted to its original function. The dining room's carved stone chimneypiece is probably from around 1620; it was originally from a merchant's house in Bristol,[10] and was acquired by

↑ The family sitting room lies at the heart of the house, with deep, comfortable sofas and a warm, boldly patterned paper.

The main chimneypiece in the dining room dates to around 1620, and came originally from a merchant's house in Bristol.

the eagle-eyed antique hunter Colonel Bailey from a sale of fragments housed at Cadbury Hall, in Gloucester.

A spacious family kitchen and informal dining room have been carved out of the old kitchen and pantry area on the lower ground floor, which appeared to have hardly been used since the 1930s. Sting and Mertens together designed a new library and office space with a vaulted hall with a swooping spiral staircase to provide an ingenious link between the family kitchen and sitting room on the main ground floor. On the top floor, the builders created a large room in the roof space that serves as a sitting room for the younger members of the family. Many improvements have been made around the wider setting of the house: cottages have been restored and converted and

the stables have been rebuilt, and at the time this book went to press, Julian and Isabel Bannerman were working on a new garden in the pool area.

The architectural qualities of Lake House are enhanced by the green hills that surround it and shelter it, and the river that runs below it, forming one of the most memorable of water gardens, with banks of irises and roses dipping into the streams. Especially important is the lush, garden setting, which becomes profuse close to the house, with lawns, a labyrinth cut into a gently sloping lawn and walled enclosures filled with colour. A stepped pathway is bordered with planting on a bold scale inspired by Claude Monet's garden at Giverny. This is an idyllic place that could indeed be the subject of a painter's dream.

SEZINCOTE

On an Indian theme

SEZINCOTE (HISTORICALLY PRO-
nounced Seasoncott), in Gloucestershire,
is a rare and fascinating building. A country house, begun in 1805, of warm honey-
gold Cotswolds stone, it was conceived
and executed in the spirit of an Indian
pleasure palace. A great copper dome
almost seems to float above its pavilion-
like structure as it sits on rising ground in
a typically English landscape park. On its
west side, an elongated crescent orangery
stretches out to connect with a hexagonal
pavilion; the lost east wing once led to a
matching pavilion that housed a tented
bed for the builder of Sezincote, Sir
Charles Cockerell, created 1st Baronet
in 1809.[1] The architecture of this unusual
house was to a design by Sir Charles's
younger brother, Samuel Pepys Cockerell,
and the estate first belonged to their elder
brother, Colonel John Cockerell.

Sezincote is now home to Edward
Peake, whose grandparents, Sir Cyril
and Lady Kleinwort, bought the house
in 1945. Their daughter Susanna, with
her husband David Peake, took over in
1976, caring for both house and garden
for twenty-five years. Edward now lives
at Sezincote with his wife Camilla, while
his sister Katharine Loyd runs the estate.
Having travelled in the East, Edward
discovered his family home held new
resonances, and the Tented Pavilion
now hosts a fortnightly Sufi meditation
group. He appreciates how deeply his
Sufi friends 'respond to the Islamic and
Hindu architecture as well as the peaceful spirituality of the garden, its temple,
pools and streams'.[2]

Visitors have been intrigued and
delighted by the house and garden since
it was first built. John Neale in volume VI

↓ An unforgettable view of Sezincote from the south-west; the house was begun in 1805 and inspired by Indian models. Built for Sir Charles Cockerell, it was designed by his brother Samuel Pepys Cockerell, with advice from the artist Thomas Daniell, who had travelled extensively in India.

of *The Beauties of England and Wales* (1823) described it as being 'in the style of the splendid palaces of the east. The grounds are varied and beautiful, and the whole laid out with very great taste and judgement'.[3] In 1828, local parson Reverend Francis Witts made an excursion and described it as 'striking and picturesque, after a Hindu model, the tomb of Hyder Ali, and the first view of the house, conservatory, flower garden, bank of wood etc is very pleasing'.[4] Author Evelyn Waugh came in 1930 and thought it all 'quite lovely … Regency Indian style like Brighton Pavilion only everything in Cotswold stone instead of plaster … The most lovely view in England'.[5] It was memorably hymned by John Betjeman in his Oxford memoir, *Summoned by Bells* (1960), in which he recalls visiting his undergraduate friend John Dugdale,

whose family bought Sezincote in 1884: 'Down the drive, under the early yellow leaves of oaks … the bridge, the waterfall, the Temple Pool and there they burst on us, the onion domes'.[6]

Colonel John Cockerell was a 'nabob' who had been Quartermaster General in India under Lord Cornwallis; his architect brother Samuel Pepys Cockerell was a pupil of Sir Robert Taylor and later surveyor to the East India Company. Charles Cockerell rose from being a clerk to the East India Company to principal of the Calcutta bank of Cockerell, Trail & Co. Thus the form of Sezincote reflects the family's Indian careers and wealth from that service.[7]

Sezincote lies close to Daylesford, another house designed by S.P. Cockerell, in 1793, for Warren Hastings, former Governor General of Bengal.

→ The finely detailed Mughal-style pavilion, which terminates the curved orangery wing to the south of the house.

It seems Hastings' agent William Walford helped Colonel John build up his land purchases.[8] Cockerell wrote to Walford in 1797: 'I have many conceits and fancies in regard to Seasoncote for a residence ... plans for all the grounds, and the furnishing and finishing of the house'.[9]

He planned to replace a small, damp, probably seventeenth-century house and it may possibly have been his idea to replace it with one in the style of the continent where he had lived and worked, and to live there with his Indo-Portuguese mistress, Estuarta, with whom he is thought to have had four children, then living with his sister in India.[10] This never transpired because Colonel John died in 1798.[11]

↑ The south elevation of the house, with its central canted bay on the principal first floor, suggests a 'pleasure palace' taken from an Indian miniature painting.

↓ The elegant principal neoclassical staircase designed by S.P. Cockerell and decorated in stony pinks by John Fowler in the 1950s.

Colonel John left the estate to his brothers and sister, but Charles Cockerell bought them out in 1801. In a stroke of genius, Charles and S.P. Cockerell involved artist Thomas Daniell, who had travelled widely in India, in their plans.[12] Daniell's unparalleled knowledge meant that he could provide Indian detailing and motifs, while Cockerell designed an essentially neoclassical house, adding Daniell's minarets, 'peacock-tail' windows, jali-work railings, pavilions and decoration (both Hindu and Muslim) on the entrance.

The copper dome was originally painted white and was Mughal in spirit, as are the first-floor curvilinear hood-moulding and arches, while the recessed

← ← The master bedroom, with curtains and draped bed designed by John Fowler. This room was the original 'Eating Room'.

double-height entrance (an 'iwan') was distinctive of Islamic Central Asia although also taken up by the Mughals in India. The house seems to have been complete by 1811, with additional accommodation for Sir Charles's growing family, and the handsome curved orangery to the south connecting with an octagonal pavilion. A walkway to the north terminated in an octagonal Tent Room where Sir Charles had his bed.

Thomas Daniell also designed the elegant Indian bridge and garden temple pool with a Coade figure of the Hindu sun god Surya.[13] Some flavour of the relationship between Charles Cockerell and Thomas Daniell is illustrated by a letter of January 1811 in which Thomas Daniell wrote of the placing of the Brahmin bulls on the bridge: 'I am dreadfully alarmed about the Brahminy Bulls – because I am certain they cannot be better placed – could Viswakarma, the Artist of the Gods, of Hindoos take a peek at Sezincote, he would say let the bulls remain where they are'.[14]

Landscape designer Humphry Repton was 'consulted by the proprietor of Sesincot, in Gloucestershire, where he wished to introduce the Gardening and Architecture which he had seen in India' in 1804–5 and appears to have suggested both the conservatory walkway to the south and the fort-like stables on the hill. He wrote of how he learnt about the Hindu style directly from his client and 'through the accurate sketches and drawings made on the spot by my ingenious friend Mr T. Daniell, I was pleased at having discovered new sources of beauty and variety'.[15] Repton was so thrilled by the unfolding house that he persuaded the Prince Regent to visit before he

embarked on the remodelling of the Brighton Pavilion (although that was done by John Nash, and the Prince had already in 1803 commissioned Indian-style stables to designs by William Porden).[16] The Prince of Wales's feathers, under the eaves on the south front, commemorate his visit to Sezincote in 1807.[17]

Repton provided a rough sketch for a coachman's house and stables on the hill in the manner of an Indian fort, which were built and provide a striking eye-catcher.[18] After 1818, monumental gateways and lodges were designed by Sir Charles's nephew, Charles Robert Cockerell, the latter with curvilinear roofs adapted from the model of a Bengal hut.[19] Around 1827, he added further guest bedrooms and new offices to the house, replacing the walkway to the Tent Room.

Part of the surprise and charm of Sezincote is the interior of the main house, which is purely classical – Greek Revival – in spirit. It seems there was never any thought of creating a neo-Indian interior and inside work continued into the 1820s. A low-ceilinged hall leads to a handsome staircase that rises to a half landing under the dome in two curving flights, then ascends to the first-floor *piano nobile* in a single flight. The finest room is the great Saloon (originally a ballroom) with its coved ceiling. A segmental vaulted room to the east was the original 'Eating Room' and is now a master bedroom.[20]

The quality of the interiors today belongs to the post-war period. After 1945, Sir Cyril and Lady Kleinwort restored the house with the architect Jeremy Benson, and furnished it with great style, decorating principal rooms with advice from the mid-1950s from

→ Muralist George Oakes decorated the walls of the dining room with views inspired by the paintings of Thomas Daniell. The scheme, completed in 1982, was commissioned by Lady Kleinwort as a welcome gift when she handed over the house to her daughter Susanna (Suki) and son-in-law David Peake.

← The walls of the drawing room are hung in a warm yellow silk, with gilded decoration on the coved ceiling. This was the original ballroom.

→ Details of the fine curtains that give the house so much of its character, with their fringes and tassels. *Clockwise from top left*: the master bedroom; the drawing room; drawing room tassels; the curtain on the tented bed.

←← Draped curtains in theatrical Regency spirit frame the garden views from the great canted bow window of the first-floor drawing room.

John Fowler, whose schemes are mostly still *in situ* in the hall, staircase hall, Saloon and two principal bedrooms.[21] Edward Peake observes: 'My grand-mother fell in love with the romance of Sezincote, and became well known to the furniture dealers of London as she redecorated a room at a time'.[22]

The entrance hall was painted with yellow 'dragged' walls and hung with yellow corduroy curtains.[23] The skirting boards were marbled by the painter Jean Hornak and exotic lamps were adapted from antique Chinese tea canisters. The Kleinworts and Peakes over the years managed to buy back six of a sequence of seven painted views of the house and park commissioned by Sir Charles Cockerell from Thomas Daniell, which now hang in this room.[24] The staircase hall was painted dusty pink (it took two layers to get it right) and framed tapestries – the framing modelled on an example at Cholmondeley Castle in Cheshire – hung on the walls to break up the surfaces.

The Saloon is described in Martin Wood's book on Fowler as 'one of the most magnificent rooms that John ever decorated'.[25] The walls were hung with yellow silk moiré and neoclassical drapes form a continuous sequence around the bow – Chamberlain and Mason made up the curtains using an illustration from *Ackermann's Repository* as a reference point. The trimming of bullion fringe and bobble tassels was designed by Fowler and custom-made by Clarke's. Typical of the furniture Lady Kleinwort acquired for the house are a set of six 1770s Madras-region sandalwood chairs with cane seats, veneered with ivory and detailed with black lacquer and gilt.

The master bedroom is picked out in three shades of blue, with a large cano-pied shantung silk bed by John Mason. Stanley Peters helped with the Oriental bedroom in which the tent poles from Charles Cockerell's Pavilion bedroom were used to create a new bed, alongside a *trompe-l'oeil* mural by Geoffrey Ghin.[26] When Lady Kleinwort handed over the house to her daughter Susanna (Suki) and son-in-law David Peake in the late 1970s, she commissioned a work by muralist George Oakes as a welcome gift. Completed in 1982 on the walls of the dining room, the scheme features Indian-inspired views that draw on the paintings of Thomas Daniell.

From the 1950s, Lady Kleinwort also brought in Graham Stuart Thomas, gar-dens adviser to the National Trust, to help create gardens sympathetic to the house, work continued by the Peakes.[27] Above the canal is a wildflower meadow with Persian quince and damask roses, and Stuart Thomas introduced the deep sinu-ous borders of planting and a patchwork of perennials. The otherworldly quality of these gardens is appropriate to the unique atmosphere of the house and its landscape.

→ *clockwise from top left:* a detail of the entrance hall with a chair in the chinoiserie style; the modern tented bedroom in the east-facing octagonal pavilion; a painting of the house by Thomas Daniell in the entrance hall; the original tented and domed bed from the octagonal pavilion now in the main house.

ON
COLOUR

This selection of twenty houses, from the grandest interiors to artistic country retreats, illustrates how our changing ideas about colour have been used to enhance character and tone. For a long time, colours were part of a recognised hierarchy, and were chosen to express fashion and affluence, but the houses in this book reveal a more varied and inventive spread of influences and ideas. Tradition and modernity blend into a world of light and comfort, as colours are inflected by history or employed as a setting for art. Colour sings in Hugo Rittson Thomas's photographs, from the memorable dark grey-blue of the drawing room at Haddon to the pink-washed bedroom at Ham Court, from the glittering saloon at Sezincote to the flock-hung dining room at Pitshill. On walls, textiles and furnishings, colour invites attention. Jocasta Innes, champion of historically inspired paint effects, called colour 'the most memorable feature of all the rooms and interiors I have enjoyed and envied', and said that decisions about colour are 'the first question that preoccupies me when I have a room, or several rooms, to decorate'.[1]

The earliest pigments, discussed in Book VII of Vitruvius's first-century BC treatise on architecture, were rooted in nature: earth and clay gave chalk, ochre, sienna and umber; minerals were also used, such as the metal ore cinnabar, which produced vermilion.[2] Vitruvius evidently thought of colour as a significant part of architecture, and colours modelled on the natural tints of stone and timber have played an important role in the interiors of English grand houses. In the 1660s, gentleman architect Sir Roger Pratt wrote: 'All painting ought to imitate the natural colour of the most excellent things in their kind'.[3] As the architectural historian, natural-paint specialist, and interior designer Edward Bulmer suggests, we need to 'follow the money: historically speaking, colour choices made in country houses were a way of projecting a message about your wealth and sophistication. Stone colours were used in the entrance hall and corridors, and all the expensive colours and furnishings would be concentrated in the rooms of parade'.[4] These decisions were about enhancing architectural space and

→ A corner of the Arts and Crafts–style
Voewood in Norfolk, with a new colour scheme
introduced by current owner Simon Finch and
hand-painted by artist Annabel Grey.

light, and Pratt argued that 'the colours of the rooms ought not to be taken at random but chosen according to the much or little light, or space of the places etc.'.[5]

In grand sixteenth-century interiors, colour was often projected through movable elements: magnificent woven tapestry, painted cloth or embroidered hangings that travelled with the household. Hangings created surfaces and backdrops rippling with colour, figures and images of nature in the form of Arcadian or hunting scenes. Wainscot (panelling) provided warmth and might be elaborately painted to resemble inlay or marble.[6] According to William Harrison's 'Historicall Description of the Island of Britayne', ceilings were often of a 'delectable whitenesse'.[7]

Paint colours were used to help project a sense of sequence and hierarchy – even procession – through the rooms of a house. The interiors of Ham House were painted in 1637–39 for the William Murray, 1st Earl of Dysart: the entrance hall and staircase were grained in imitation of walnut, and the joinery gilded; the former dining room was painted throughout, wainscot and all, in a deep 'fair blew' (blue verditer) with some details gilded, under a white ceiling.[8] The cost of this expensive oil colour would have been immediately understood alongside the quality of furnishings and finishes.

Wainscot was commonly marbled or grained in imitation of various woods, such as olive, yew, walnut and cedar. Mention of such woods in house accounts might well refer to just a colour: cedar, cinnamon, timber, umber, walnut tree or white.[9] A popular colour for wainscot was green, but pale grey and pale blue are also encountered.[10] If not muralled with stories from Ovid's *Metamorphoses* and the like, ceilings seemed to be mostly white; Richard Neve, in *The City and Country Purchaser's and Builder's Dictionary* (1703), referenced 'the Plaistered Ceilings so much used in England, beyond all other Countries, make by their whiteness the Rooms so much Lightsomer'.[11] The reflection of light – whether from daylight, candles or open fires – was important and, from the mid-seventeenth century, Oriental lacquer panels, known as 'Japan', were highly prized for their reflective qualities.

Palladian taste favoured stuccoed walls that were habitually painted in white or stone colours. Mrs Lybbe Powys described the hugely admired sculpture gallery at Holkham Hall as painted a 'dead white, with ornaments of gilding': here 'dead' meant a flat finish with a final coat of turpentine. Doors were increasingly made of imported mahogany, or painted 'mahogany' or 'chocolate' to resemble exotic wood.[12] In the mid-eighteenth century a principal saloon or drawing room was often hung in a richly coloured crimson damask or caffoy, using the silk as a permanent fitting framed between a chair rail and plaster cornice, with the joinery and stucco painted white. The layered effect of shimmering backdrops – damask-silk draped curtains and matching silk-upholstered furniture, with gilding applied to the carved parts – was magnificence itself. Considered the foremost in a system of colours derived from heraldry, red was associated with Mars, nobility and state; green with Venus, and therefore often used in bedrooms; and blue with Jupiter, the 'third in traditional colour hierarchy'.[13]

Olive and pearl were popular wall colours, along with cream and stone; these were used even in grand interiors where they might be ornamented with gilded detailing.[14] Brighter colours, including blue and yellow, seem to have been the result of French influence, and in the 1740s a fashionable green could cost twelve times as much as a 'common' colour like stone.[15] In the seventeenth century printed wallpapers were produced in England and were available in single sheets as an alternative to textile hangings. Wallpapers increased in popularity, especially for more intimate areas such as bedrooms and dressing rooms. Hand-painted Chinese panels – often referred to as 'India' paper because they were imported by the East India Company – were highly popular and favoured for their virtuosity and colour range.[16] Between 1740 and 1790, most country houses boasted a room furnished with these painted Chinese wallpapers, which were considered thrillingly exotic and cosmopolitan. Even today, they have a transporting effect when encountered in the bedroom at Court of Noke, for example.

Mid-eighteenth-century interest in the Roman Antique encouraged a richer palette of colours, as seen in the interiors of James Paine, Sir William Chambers and Robert Adam. Adam's work at houses such as Syon set a new standard of magnificence. Walls were painted in pale greens or pinks – colours associated with the interiors of the ruins of Herculaneum and Pompeii – and often in combinations of the two, with yellows and blues also seen. Entrance and staircase halls tended towards plain colours such as stone, but the rooms of parade showed increasing richness and intensity,[17] enhanced by ceilings 'coloured in the stile of the Ancients'.[18] As time went on, Adam favoured a 'tinted' ceiling, rather than a densely ornamented one, no doubt partly for reasons of cost. But Ian Bristow has suggested that contemporary aesthetic theory may have led towards a preference for paler colours, in response to Edmund Burke's *Philosophical Enquiry* (1757) and discussions of beauty and the sublime. As Chambers noted: 'First, the colours of beautiful bodies must not be dusky or muddy, but clean and fair … Those which seem most appropriated to beauty, are the milder of every sort: light greens; soft blues; weak whites; pink reds; and violets'.[19]

The Regency was a period of varied stylistic enthusiasms and a taste for ever-stronger colours in principal rooms. Interior styles continued to be informed by archaeological discoveries and art-historical knowledge, including those from Pompeiian, Turkish, Saracenic, Indian and Chinese, as well as historic French styles and native Gothic and Elizabethan.[20] Marbling, associated with Egyptian, Etruscan and Chinese-inspired interiors,[21] became popular again from the early 1800s. Nonetheless, many rooms were still painted in traditional natural and neutral colours used since the early eighteenth century. As one 1807 house painter put it: 'the most fashionable colours for Plaster walls are The Stone and Gray Colours'.[22]

Throughout the nineteenth century, designers and patrons selected deeper, richer colours, such as the reds found on ancient Roman walls, where they were used as the ground colour for mural painting. Deep red was considered especially suited to picture galleries, as seen in the picture gallery at Attingham,[23] and it was also favoured for libraries. As a contemporary author noted: 'crimson [is] a colour that agrees with books and their bindings'.[24]

More thought was also being given to how colours worked. Decorative artist David Ramsay Hay advised that rooms facing north or east should be decorated in warm tones, and those facing south or west in more cool colours. Humphry Repton thought drawing rooms should be 'the richest and most decorated of all the Rooms', and Hay mentioned their need to create an atmosphere of 'vivacity, gaiety and light cheerfulness'.[25] Decorators were starting to balance the colours of walls against the vibrant hues of textiles. For bedrooms, Hay suggested that 'a light, clear, and cheerful style of colouring is the most appropriate', and he noted that 'a greater degree of contrast may be here admitted … as the bed and window curtains form a sufficient mass to balance a tint of equal intensity upon the walls'.[26]

In the early nineteenth century, the availability of wallpaper was further transformed after improvements in manufacturing allowed it to be produced in rolls. Colour fields also changed, not least with the popularity of the high Gothic as championed by A.W.N. Pugin, with its simple, bright, heraldic colours resonating with the strong patterning of Gothic floor tiles.[27] William Morris shared some common ground during the 1860s, when his block-printed wallpapers and woven textiles were rooted in Gothic art, but in the 1870s he moved towards bolder natural foliage and damask patterns.[28]

In the early twentieth century, many colours shifted towards simplification under the influence of Arts and Crafts restraint; alongside this was a representation of 'Old English' that also appears to have derived from Dutch interior paintings (as reflected in *Country Life* photography of this era), or an increasing admiration for eighteenth-century interiors. There was also a major move away from professional decorating firms to the new influence of the individual 'interior decorator'. In the 1920s and '30s, the 'country-house' look associated with decorator Nancy Lancaster was one that featured warm colours applied in many coats by her experienced professional painter, Mr Kick.[29] Lancaster, who became owner of Colefax and Fowler in 1948, was already one of the great names of interior decoration, and, along with her ally John Fowler, had been part of 'a romantic revival using rich colours and furniture of a sophisticated type'.[30]

Hugely influential during the post-war period, Fowler had a very practical approach and 'a painter's eye for colour'.[31] He advised many country-house owners who wanted to achieve a combination of elegance and comfort that suited the architectural context; the Sezincote rooms in this volume capture some of the best of his surviving interiors. Tom Helme – Fowler's assistant and successor as the National Trust's adviser on decoration – acquired Farrow & Ball, and his focus on traditional colours stimulated interest in finding tones that suited historic interiors while also bringing warmth. Patrick Baty of Paper and Paints is the author of *The Anatomy of Colour* (2017) and has helped extend understanding of historic colours as specified in historic contracts and through advanced mircoscopic paint analysis.[32] Edward Bulmer, owner of Court of Noke, has recently championed natural paint colours with a range based on his knowledge of the historic country-house interior.

Since the 1980s, there has been a cycle of interest among historically informed designers, turning towards cooler, plainer interiors and then back to warmer shades and more variety, especially between rooms. But twenty-first-century colour choices also tend to give interiors a lightness and spaciousness inflected by an almost modernistic taste and a greater degree of informal living. Interior designer Nina Campbell observes that 'in the 1980s there was a real interest in mixing colour and pattern, and a search for warmth, and then there was a reaction and everything went very cool and grey. Rich colour has returned in recent years, but I think is used with more freedom'.[33] Her daughter Rita Konig, whose North Farm is featured in this volume, suggests that 'it takes confidence to use colour well, but it can bring real joy to an interior'.[34] Bulmer says that while the inspiration of the past remains strong, it now allows for a much greater freedom of choice while drawing on a reliable traditional palette: 'Light is a critical determinant in the interior, but perhaps the issue is that colour is second to tonality in the country-house interior. It is the relationship of all the painted and dyed surfaces and natural materials, stone and wood, that really matters'.[35]

→ A detail of the 'new' north range added by
W.D. Caröe when he remodelled the house in 1907–8,
expressing an Arts and Crafts delight in traditional
materials but realised in an almost sculptural way.

VANN

The essence of English

VANN IS A SPELLBINDING HOUSE that lies on the Surrey–Sussex border close to the villages of Hambledon and Chiddingfold. It is the picture of an English ideal, hidden among oak-filled woods and rolling pastures. Its curiously blunt monosyllabic name is thought to derive from the word 'fen' – it was once spelled 'Ffann'. On the east side, the core of the house is discernible as a low, probably mid-sixteenth-century range (c. 1540) adapted in the late sixteenth century with the insertion of a brick chimney, and a major addition around 1690 to the south.[1] This rambling though not over-large house was acquired about 110 years ago by a remarkable Edwardian architect, William Douglas Caröe, who remodelled and extended it in 1907–8 into a quiet masterpiece of English architecture. This drew as much on an admiration for the simplicity of Surrey barns, cottages and farmhouses as on any grander notion of the country house, yet a country house it is: manorial, modest, emerging from the landscape.

Caröe was a highly rational figure, but also one who had imbibed deeply of the romantic idealism of the late nineteenth century, which venerated the aesthetic of old English architecture. He was born near Liverpool in 1857, the younger son of the Danish consul in the city, and had been articled to Edmund Kirby of Liverpool before becoming the trusted assistant to John Loughborough Pearson, the great church architect.[2] In 1895 Caröe was appointed architect to the Ecclesiastical Commissioners and as a result was the architect of the

← The north-west corner of the house, which shows the spirited and artistic approach to domestic design in the early 1900s, with a playful juxtaposition of corner windows, gables and chimneys.

Old Palace in Canterbury from 1897 to 1901, the remarkable Bishop's Palace at Southwell and the Ecclesiastical Commissioners building at No. 1 Millbank, London.[3]

The desire to have a house in the country appears to have come more from Caröe's wife, Grace Rendall, who, like many educated people of her generation, had a taste for medieval and Tudor architecture and looked at other historic sites before they chose Vann.[4] A cousin, Monty Rendall, Headmaster of Winchester College, later employed Caröe to work on his country house formed from the remaining fragment of medieval Butley Priory in Suffolk. At first the Caröes rented Vann, but on a lease that allowed them to extend, and only purchased the freehold in 1930. Grace Caröe was a sophisticated figure, who dressed in exotic clothes, spoke several languages and had a strong interest in the theatre. She also hand-stitched many of the curtains and cushions for the house, which were adapted from Turkoman tent bands.[5]

Vann remains in Caroe family hands (W.D. Caröe's successors do not use the umlaut in Caroe, of which W.D. was rather proud), and it has been, in part, a dynasty of architects: W.D. Caröe's second son Alban, his grandson Martin and his great-grandson Oliver Caroe have all been architects – the latter is the current Surveyor to the Fabric of St Paul's Cathedral. All the Caröe architects cite Vann as a deep source of relevance to their practice and as a healing refuge and a place of renewal. But the house and garden express equally as much about the women of the family. In addition to Grace, there was also her daughter-in-law Gwendolen, daughter of the eminent scientist Sir William Bragg, who arrived here in the challenging post-war years

↑ The north range was effectively merged with the mid-sixteenth-century timber-framed house seen to the left.

→→ The pergola, designed by W.D. Caröe, carries the eye out from the house to the field beyond: always lush and green, it is a favoured eating spot and another corner where garden and nature merge.

and brought with her the instincts of an artist and a poet, managing the house as a weekend retreat from London, with her daughter Lucy, later Lady Adrian; and then Martin Caroe's wife, Mary, a doctor and mother of five, who has cared for and nurtured the house and garden for more than fifty years.

The layered, textured house, with its brick, stone and timber-framed elements, its patchwork of clay-tiled roofs, has an almost sculptural feel, and W.D. Carōe's extensions to the older house were robust but also sensitive. He added a low-spreading range across the north end of the house, with a master bedroom suite and a bathroom, and opened up the space within the house (removing subdivisions). The new wing was aligned with a pergola running towards the pond, with an apsidal seating area facing the water. A new parlour was created in the old house at the centre of the composition, and a fine Jacobean plasterwork ceiling of about 1620, saved from a town house in Llandovery, called Neuadd Newyd, was introduced.

In 1908–9 Carōe converted the traditional hay barn into a handsome oak-boarded great-hall-type social space, with a wide inglenook and a gallery overlooking it all. This was a splendid room that was intended for performances, including an elaborate staging of John Milton's *The Masque of Comus*, music parties, fancy dress and billiards. It echoes in some way the barn theatre at Ellen Terry's house at Smallhythe, in Kent. The Dolmetsch family gave a concert in the garden; actor-manager Donald Wolfit was an early protégé of Grace's. This was a house to be enjoyed in the full Edwardian spirit of artistic and social confidence.

The long corridor between the staircase hall and the barn was ingeniously modelled from the old open cart sheds. The parlour was entered from the staircase hall, and with the link corridor to the barn, in effect contributed to an open-plan design, at about the same time as its invention was ascribed to Frank Lloyd Wright in around 1909.[6] Later, Carōe designed some movable panelling that could be used to enclose the parlour from the chills of open-plan living in winter.

The warm, panelled interiors have a strong sense of Englishness – of oak, plaster, pictures, books, pewter plates on shelves – and the entrance hall is enhanced with casts of classical friezes. Carōe also installed seventeenth-century-style lamps of his own design in the barn, reminiscent of the work of Charles Ashbee, and lit by 50-volt electricity. The bedrooms all have views out to the garden, and the oak and beech woods that surround the house. Hints of the healthy outdoor ideals of the Edwardian era can still be read in the first-floor north bathroom, which was originally fitted out with an extraordinary mahogany-clad 'bath-temple' with multiple showerheads and taps (since removed, but some of the fittings and taps survive *in situ*). The selection of such a temple to hygiene was consistent with Carōe's health-conscious approach: the dressing room has a vaulted ceiling with a rail across it so that he could perform his daily callisthenics and pull-ups.[7]

It is quite clear what is old and what is new. Architectural historian Tim Brittain-Catlin has recently argued for recognition of the originality of such buildings, and regards Vann as 'the outstanding example of an old-and-new house'.[8]

He notes how Caröe was deeply interested in timber detailing, but in working sympathetically with the old produced something distinctively new. As Brittain-Catlin writes: 'the whole building became a homogenous fusing of the old and the new, of the rational with the historical'.

The style of the chimneypieces and doorcases floated between the simple character of Arts and Crafts–inspired Tudor and echoes of a kind of rustic baroque. These fine details were further enhanced by the ceramics and Persian and Tibetan textiles that were spread through the house. In the 1930s Caröe designed Latomia, a large villa overlooking the sea in Kyrenia, Cyprus, and some

of his distinctive furniture designed for that house returned to Vann after his death.

Martin Caroe did some work to the house in around 1961 for his parents, including a new glazed screen and door in limed oak facing south, bringing in more light to the domestic quarters and giving direct access to the garden from the kitchen. Mary Caroe recalls that he said it was so his mother could feel as if she was in the garden when she was cooking. Martin also created a breakfast room in the former servants' hall.[9]

Martin and Mary Caroe moved into the house in 1969, but it was not until the early 1980s that they could do much

↑ The former barn was turned into a room for entertaining, with a piano, a billiard table and a gallery level, which provided a stage for family and other amateur performances, over an inglenook fireplace. Hung with Persian and Tibetan textiles, the room retains its original light fittings designed by W.D. Caröe.

→ The corridor linking the main staircase hall and parlour with the former barn can be divided off into sections by curtains.

to make the house more comfortable, installing new heating, and by Martin's further remodelling the original kitchen in a distinctly Scandinavian flavour, to create a modern living family kitchen. The scullery and coke room then became a working kitchen (known as the 'summer kitchen') and the former servants' hall was changed into a family 'snug' with cork-lined walls. Mary recalls that quite a lot of furniture was divided among different members of the family in the 1980s, but pieces from her parents and uncle filled the gaps ('but Martin would not let any mahogany into Vann, he said it was an oak house').[10] In 1990 their son, Oliver, newly qualified as an architect, helped remodel these key living spaces, removing an old boiler to enlarge the inner kitchen and installing a new Aga in the

↑ The seat within the bay window of the parlour on the east front of the house, with recently installed crewel-work curtains. The room today doubles as family drawing room and dining room.

↓ The inglenook fireplace, with built-in seats, provides a focus of light and warmth in the parlour. Paintings by Julian Trevelyan and Elizabeth Blackadder hang on either side of the fireplace.

main family kitchen. All the new joinery in oak is in the spirit of the older house.

W.D. and Grace Caröe began a remarkable garden, which merges with the Surrey landscape with a softness that echoes the best of Arts and Crafts ideals. Grace Caröe was interested in aesthetic effect, while W.D. Caröe had the design vision, including the pergola that connects the house to the garden.

A water garden designed with advice from Gertrude Jekyll was laid out in 1911, linking a succession of small ponds fed by the cascade from the dammed quarter-acre pond by the house, and crossed by stone paths and bridges. It was all banked with 1,500 water-loving plants supplied by Jekyll from her own nursery at Munstead, in Surrey, and it seems likely she gave further advice

→ A Surrey scene: a glimpse of the house and pergola framed by an oak tree from across the natural swimming pond.

about planting.[11] Gwendolen Caroe took a great interest in the flowers at Vann, and passed this passion on to her son Martin, who was devoted to the garden. Mary recalls how they had to simplify planting to make it all more manageable, but that this introduced new possibilities.

To the north, the stream enters the garden and runs through the 1909 Yew Walk in a rill flanked by drystone Bargate walls, originally a rose garden but replanted by Martin and Mary: 'Martin had a superb architect's eye for plants, and we replanted this walk with foliage and bulbs so that it has colour from January to December. In 1992, by way of reducing the large vegetable garden, Martin made a new border 60-feet-by-18-feet, and I suggested we plant it with Jekyll-inspired

colours, hot reds to cool blues and yellows'. The stream today flows down to the White Garden, which is a blanket of snowdrops in February followed by narcissi, white fritillaries and martagon lilies, before continuing into the coppiced woodland beyond.

Among the innovations of Mary's decades of stewardship is the increased area of wild flower plantings, snake's head fritillaries, lady's smock, wood anemones, cowslips and forget-me-nots. Vann is still hugely admired by visitors from around the world, and many are struck by the curious blending of the boundaries between the designed and the natural, in which the house and garden seem almost to merge. It is an idea that would have appealed greatly to W.D. Caröe and his wife Grace.[12]

↑ Textiles and pottery stand on the piano in the barn room against a background of limed oak boards.

2 ENGLISH

CLASSICS

SMEDMORE
Hidden Dorset manor

KIMMERIDGE BAY, IN DORSET, IS one of those hidden parts of England that seems uniquely untouched by the modern world. Smedmore, the family home of writer Dr Philip Mansel, sits in stately remoteness just above the bay, looking out to sea, but sheltered by the particular form of the landscape.[1] With a mid-eighteenth-century frontage of pearl-grey Portland stone, Smedmore is settled in the greenness of the surrounding landscape as still as a poem. Appropriately for the house of a writer – part of an inheritance that he cherishes and protects for future generations of the family – it has moved other writers to passages of memorable, resonant praise.

The historian Alfred Leslie Rowse, on his visit to Sir Arthur Bryant, who leased the house for a time in the 1950s, wrote of the house as being 'very virginal and lovely, waiting at the end of the road beyond which there is no further. It is a dream of a place'.[2] Lord David Cecil also felt there was something beguiling in this house and wrote in *Some Dorset Country Houses* (1985) that the main rooms here are 'in the highest degree welcoming and reassuring; but they also stir the imagination. They are full of picturesque ghosts', hinting at the layered quality of the building as much as the portraits and furnishings.[3]

Dr Mansel is a well-known author and historian of France and the Ottoman Empire, whose critically acclaimed biography *King of the World: The Life of Louis XIV* was published in 2020. He took over the house and 1,800-acre estate from his father, Major John Clavell Mansel,

← ← Smedmore, Dorset, is an older house refronted in the later eighteenth century in pale Portland stone with great bow windows that offer oblique views to the sea.

in 1989. He has hosted many artists and literary figures, all of whom are touched by Smedmore's quiet English reserve and coastal setting.[4]

Dr Mansel has overseen the planting of new woodland and has also championed the rescue of an 1830s folly, the derelict Clavell Tower, built by an eccentric clerical relation, which was then about to collapse into the sea. The building was

dismantled and rebuilt further inland and now is an exhilarating Landmark Trust holiday retreat. The structure was once visited by a young Thomas Hardy and inspired *The Black Tower* (1975) by novelist P.D. James.[5]

Smedmore is a house of different ages. It has grown from a small seventeenth-century gentry house to its current – still essentially eighteenth-century – form, but it has been in the same family hands

↑ A room with a view: the bow window in the drawing room is hung with plates and prints but no curtains, just painted shutters to shut out the night.

since 1391, when sold by the last de Smedmore. Thomas Gerard's 1620s manuscript history of Dorset – published in John Coker's *A Survey of Dorsetshire* (1732)[6] – referred to 'a little newe House at Smedmore and beautified it with pleasant Gardens', built by 'Sir William Clavile, descended of antient Gentrie'.

The building of this house was in fact, despite his ancient lineage, part of a

rather daring, if doomed, commercial enterprise. Clavell wanted to mine for alum and use natural shale for glassmaking (and even attempted to extract salt from seawater). It was all an embarrassing flop, and after 1623 his property was handed over to trustees, who sold much of the land to pay off his debts. Smedmore House, however, was settled on him for life and, on his death, passed to a hardworking farmer kinsman, Roger Clavell of Winfrith Newburgh.

His grandson, Edward Clavell, inherited the property and was luckily able to draw on the wealth of his father, Walter Clavell, East India merchant and administrator – for a time the 'Chief of the factories in the Bay of Bengal'.[7] Walter had inherited the small Dorset family estate in 1676, but never returned to live at Smedmore, leaving it to his younger son Edward, born in Cossimbazar, educated at St Paul's and briefly an MP, to do the honours – and indeed to serve as High Sheriff of Dorset in 1705.[8] Edward married well (twice), first to Jane, the daughter of merchant-prince Sir Edward Littleton, the East India Company's governor in Bengal. After her death, he was married again, in 1717, to Elizabeth Damer – an important link with one of the rising families of the county.

Edward Clavell, perhaps celebrating his appointment to the sheriffdom, updated the house and remodelled what is now the garden front to the south-west (but appears to have been the entrance at that time).[9] This work was in a then very up-to-date style, with tall windows in bolection-moulded surrounds and the main door framed by a projecting cornice supported on finely detailed brackets linked to the carved surround of the first-floor window above. The wainscoted room at the centre of this front – always called the Cedar Room – may have been the entrance hall, with a parlour to either side, only one of which survives, with an ornamented cornice and a bolection-moulded chimneypiece. The handsome principal oak staircase of around 1700 lies just behind the Cedar

Room. Windows of the early seventeenth century can still be seen from the internal courtyard. The stable block behind seems to have been added around 1720.

But this is not the full story, as the next generation carried on with improvements. Edward's second son, George, inheriting from his older brother in 1744, created the stately new entrance front on the north-west side, with double-height bow windows giving wonderful seaward views. The architect is not known but the work bears close comparison with several local houses, so no doubt was in the hands of one of the expert mason families of the region, such as the Bastard brothers of Blandford, who took on architectural design and construction.[10]

The overall composition is very calm and settled. The central entrance door is framed with Ionic-order engaged columns with a triangular pediment, and leads into the generous entrance hall (known as 'The Outer Hall') with an elegant dining room to the north and cheerfully light drawing room to the south. All these rooms have walls that are panelled in plaster frames and ornate modillion cornices, although the ceilings are plain. A new stone kitchen with a Venetian window, and all the usual associated domestic offices to either side lit by simpler Gothic arched windows, seems to have been added in about 1760.

The estate passed to the Reverend John Clavell, who built the round tower on the cliffs. He died in 1833 without a will and there was a court case over the inheritance between his farm manager, 'old Barnes', and his niece Louisa, née Pleydell, and her husband, Colonel John Mansel. The latter wrote in his diary: 'Intense anxiety evinced by all orders

→ *clockwise from top left:* a view down to the sea from the house; a classical bust on a bracket in the entrance hall; the elegant front to the garden remodelled around 1700 for merchant Edward Clavell; a detail of the marble chimneypiece in the drawing room.

of Society as to the result of the trial whether poor Smedmore shall remain in the same family it has for four centuries been or pass into the hands of a set of forgers'.[11] This Colonel Mansel brought an ebonised chair to the house, which was made by George Bullock for Napoleon in exile on St Helena, and which was presented to him after he had been garrisoned there.

In one of those chances that happen in the stories of English country houses, the best of the furniture and pictures arrived much later, in 1934, inherited by Dr Mansel's great-great-aunt, Kitty Mansel, aunt of his grandfather Major Rhys Mansel, from the collection of her aunt Lady Elizabeth Villiers, heiress to the last Earls of Athlone: the 1st Earl, Godart de Ginkel, was a general under

↑ The bow window of the main bedroom looking out towards Kimmeridge Bay.

↓ The dining room is painted in a pale pink,
on the advice of historic buildings expert Gervase
Jackson-Stops, and hung with more than a
hundred eighteenth-century Fürstenberg plates.

William III. This inheritance included much fine marquetry furniture, china and pictures, including the portrait after Anthony van Dyck of the children of Charles I that hangs in the drawing room and the huge bird paintings in rare painted late seventeenth-century frames.[12]

The settings for the furniture and pictures have all been tactfully improved by Dr Mansel, introducing new colour schemes in the house to bring out the quality of the 1760s interiors, as well as Middle Eastern textiles and Oriental ceramics. But so well judged are the arrangements that they have the feel of having always been there. A glance at *Country Life* photographs taken in 1934 shows how much more austere the interiors of the house appeared at that time.[13]

→ An inviting view looking through the 1760s doorcase in the dining room across the entrance hall into the drawing room. This sequence of rooms was created at the same time and is remarkably adaptable for modern entertaining.

Dr Mansel's gentle improvements include introducing the warm, buttercup yellow in the drawing room and the pale stony pink of the dining room. A friend and rococo expert, the late Gervase Jackson-Stops, suggested the dining room colour. In 2008, with advice from decorator Frouz Fartasht, Dr Mansel hung more than a hundred eighteenth-century Fürstenberg plates (made in the china factory owned by the Dukes of Brunswick) in a style of display inspired by decorative schemes in northern European rococo palaces.[14]

Dr Mansel also created the memorable Turkish Room, which adjoins the panelled Cedar Room, with blue walls and richly coloured and patterned Turkish fabrics and floor cushions. He also has established 'the War Room', a small museum dedicated to the photographs and letters of his two great-aunts who both served as nurses at the Front during the First World War for the British and then the French Red Cross.

In the more sheltered areas around the house are two acres of flower gardens, orchards and a 'Mediterranean' garden, much of which was laid out and planted by Dr Mansel's mother, Damaris, in the 1960s and '70s (work continued by gardener Glyn Morgan for the past four decades).[15] In the garden is a grave to a pet tiger who was brought to Smedmore in the 1880s but did not survive long. To the south-east of the main front lies a long ride cut through woodland, giving a dramatic oblique view of the sea. A path, marked by stone urns and obelisks, leads across fields to the bay and the poetic beauty of the ever-changing sea view.

↑ The entrance hall is cool and classical with its handsome mahogany side table framed with shield-backed hall chairs carrying the family crest.

→ A detail of the elegantly carved chimneypiece in the drawing room at Beckside House, Cumbria.

BECKSIDE HOUSE

The perfect retreat

THERE IS SOMETHING UNUSUALLY satisfying about a simple, classically composed façade between two pedimented wings: it is the essence of that vision of the Palladian form that runs as a golden thread through English architecture from the early seventeenth century. Beckside House, on the edge of the village of Barbon, on the remote north Lancashire border, is the home of distinguished herald, historian and author Dr John Martin Robinson.

The house was built in 1767 – the date is inscribed on a lintel – and is perched above a stream but neatly tucked into rising land that gives it shelter. It was extended by the addition of low wings in the late twentieth century, in a manner that perhaps enhances the historic core and includes a full-depth room with windows to the east and south, which can only be described as the Englishman's dream library.

Built of rubble stone, the front of the house is rendered and painted, with projecting stone quoins, all under a Westmorland slate roof. It has a happily formal, almost sculpted, character that represents the meeting of new metropolitan fashions with long-standing vernacular building practices. Part of the particular charm is the slightly old-fashioned quality of the elegant classical detail, especially the interior joinery, with a combination of earlier Palladian and rococo elements. The finely carved pedimented front door was modelled on a type popularised by James Gibbs's *A Book of Architecture* (1728).[1]

Certain characteristic details (especially the St Andrew's Cross between

←← The original 1767 house (possibly designed by John Hird of Cartmel) was extended for owner Dr Robinson in 1998 and 2000 with two low pedimented wings, designed after a sketch by the artist Glynn Boyd Harte.

quatrefoil heads that appears on panels of the elliptical arch in the hall) have led to the attribution to joiner turned architect John Hird of Cartmel, a regional figure typical of those who designed the plain but elegant gentleman's houses of the late eighteenth and early nineteenth centuries, and who drew on the pattern books produced by Gibbs, Batty Langley and others as sources for detail, elevation, proportion and plan. Hird worked on Sizergh Castle in Cumbria in around 1770, and provided a design for Leighton Hall in Lancashire influenced by James Paine's *Plans … of Noblemen and Gentlemen's Houses* (1767), of which he was listed as a subscriber.

The new wings at Beckside, finished in 1998 and 2000 respectively, were designed by a local architect, Michael Bottomley, following initial sketch drawings and a model by the artist Glynn Boyd Harte.[2] One wing is entirely filled with the library, a room in which Dr Robinson has written so many of his famous books; the other wing provides the essential back room of country-house life, a generous boot room – and why should it not present an elegant front to the world? This wing connects to the old wash house, which is thought to be part of the old manor house on the site.

These symmetrical single-storey wings are also a nod to their appearance in other designs by Hird, for instance, for Leighton Hall. The fenestration of the sides of the house actually appears to be arranged for such wings and so 'there is a certain inevitability about them'.[3] Each new wing has a Venetian window facing south in a blank arch underneath a pediment (echoing Hird's other designs). The central arched window

↑ A red painted chinoiserie-style bench terminates a vista in the garden.

→ The lively rococo character of the pedimented doorcase adds a special touch to the main elevation.

is given additional interest by Gothic rococo fenestration, another characteristic of designs by Hird in the 1760s. The walls of the wings are rendered and limewashed to match the original, with stone dressings in a Stanton Moor sandstone from Derbyshire, which is a close match to that used in the eighteenth century.

Beckside House was built for George Turner, a local landowner, and sold to the Gibsons – a well-established gentry family – in 1859, for whom it appears to have been a secondary house to their estate at Whelprigg in Cumbria, and quite often let.[4] This probably accounts for the lack of alterations and the perfect survival of the chimneypieces and graceful staircase of the 1760s era. Dr Robinson acquired the house from the Gibson family in 1986, and informed by his own extraordinary

↑ The library of a gentleman scholar: an elegant long room in one of the new wings is fitted out in a comfortable neoclassical style.

knowledge of English architectural history and design, every room has been decorated and furnished in a manner that epitomises traditional country-house taste, elegance and comfort combined.

Dr Robinson, a Lancashire landowner and historian, holds the distinguished offices of Maltravers Herald Extraordinary and Librarian to the Duke of Norfolk. He is also a former Vice-Chairman of the Georgian Group and is well known as a regular architectural writer for *Country Life* for over forty years, and a champion of modern classical design in Britain. He is the author of many books about English country houses and architecture, including the definitive work of leading Georgian architect, James Wyatt. His highly acclaimed book *The Latest Country Houses* (1984) was about the

↑ The intimate drawing room: the carved
chimneypiece is painted to resemble stone, and
late eighteenth- and early nineteenth-century
paintings are hung around it.

persistence of the country-house tradition, and the classical country-house tradition in particular, through the difficult post-war decades.[5]

In 2006 he produced a lively and candid memoir of his childhood and early youth, *Grass Seed in June*, that reveals his deep sense of family pride in his Lancastrian descent and his Catholicism, and the values that have shaped his interest in historic architecture and especially the eighteenth century. He recalls how arriving at Oriel College, Oxford, for postgraduate studies in the 1970s had a profound effect on him: 'late twentieth-century Oxford was a kind of architectural nirvana, an expression of my interests and enthusiasms'. While walking the streets, he realised 'it is a fallacy to claim that keeping old buildings is retrograde and ties society to an anachronistic or outdated environment. Old buildings have a chameleon character and change their appearance from century to century. They are read differently by successive generations … [and are] as much a contemporary part of the environment as brand new buildings, and are equally an expression of our own tastes and beliefs'.[6]

↑ The entrance hall in a cool stone colour is hung with deer antlers. The distinctive St Andrew's Cross detail is associated with the design work of John Hird.

↗ Looking into the master bedroom, the four-poster bed is hung with an Indian chintz pattern.

→→ In perfect Georgian style, the pale blue dining room has a cluster of prints and medallions hung above and around the chimneypiece with its distinctive carved frieze.

He has acted as consultant on the restorations of countless fine Georgian houses, beginning always from the premise that the history of the building has to be understood before decisions are made. He admits to being influenced by many of the country houses of his school friends at the Benedictine Abbey of Fort Augustus and St Andrew's University, older houses of considerable charm with 'under done up' interiors: he especially cherishes the memory of Earlshall near Fife, remodelled by Sir Robert Lorimer, with its old textiles, chintz and china.

The 1980s–90s restoration of Beckside House was exacting but deliberately conservative. The house was so unaltered, but in a poor state of repair, when he bought it in 1986, and has been gently modernised, with heating and improved plumbing, and Dr Robinson is especially proud of reoccupying the old kitchen that had been effectively abandoned for thirty years and was virtually derelict – the woodwork was painted a Naples Blue, copied from a painting by Glynn Boyd Harte.

Unsurprisingly, the principal reception rooms all bear the hallmark of the current owner's deep knowledge and judgement, a series of tones and colours that are the perfect balance to the fine mid-eighteenth-century joinery; the latter is painted mostly in simple off-whites. These carefully judged colours are also a fine backdrop to the good-quality classical furniture and portraits that Dr Robinson has either inherited or acquired for the house.

The deep red walls of the drawing room and the paler stone colour of the entrance hall bring warmth to these interiors. In the former stands an eighteenth-century Lancashire chest that his grandfather recalled rescuing from the barn of a tenant farmer. The Eating Room is in a carefully chosen pale blue against which the original 1760s – rather architectural – built-in pedimented china buffet stands out so handsomely, as do the sanguine prints bought from Christopher Lennox-Boyd's shop on the High Street in Oxford. These colours were mixed by Dr Robinson himself.

But it is the library, with its blue-green painted walls and Regency furniture, that is the triumphal space of this house. It is the easternmost of the two new wings, so well lit with windows to the east and south, under a segmental ceiling, and an open fire to the north; there are wall-to-ceiling bookcases of neoclassical inspiration echoing Samuel Wyatt, especially his design for a library at Dropmore in Buckinghamshire – the two free-standing pyramidal bookcases are Italian. The view from the south window terminates in the folly, a small temple in the manner of William Kent, designed by Dr Robinson and built by local builders to mark the millennium. This is a room for the contemplation of art and history, a place where one can sit quietly, uninterrupted. The blue-green colour was mixed by Patrick Baty and dubbed Robinson Green, based on a fragment of the original paint for the library at Heveningham Hall in Suffolk (by James Wyatt).[7] This room also serves, in the Regency manner, as the principal drawing room of the house, the place to assemble for drinks before dinner, or to return to afterwards to continue the conversation: it is the very epitome of the gentleman's library brought comfortably into the twenty-first century as a living tradition, and to prove, as Anthony Powell wrote in a novel of the same name, that 'books do furnish a room'.[8]

→ Constable Burton Hall, Yorkshire: the leather-
bound books in the library-come-billiard room speak of
country-house pastimes.

CONSTABLE BURTON HALL

Palladian simplicity

CONSTABLE BURTON HALL IS A
crisp Palladian country house, set down
on an elevated site near Leyburn, in
Yorkshire.[1] Pale, elegant, compact and
classical, it is the perfect expression of
mid-Georgian taste. Although elevated,
the house is also sheltered by mature
woodland to the north, while to the south
and east it looks out, in effect, over an
exhilarating view of treetops. There is a
low eighteenth-century courtyard beside
the house and a lime avenue leads to
extensive walled gardens further to the
north. The main entrance is on the west
front, approached by a flight of steps that
rises to the first-floor *piano nobile*.

In the sixteenth century the estate
came by marriage to the Wyvill family (descendants of Sir Humphry de
Wyvill, who arrived in England during
the Norman Conquest in 1066), and it is
owned by the same family today. In 1611
Marmaduke Wyvill, MP for Richmond, was
created 1st Baronet, but it was a later Sir
Marmaduke who was the builder of the
1760s house and who died without a direct
heir, in 1774. The baronetcy then passed to
a distant cousin, but the estate went to Sir
Marmaduke's cousin and brother-in-law
and remains with his descendants to this
day. A place where a sense of history and
hospitality intertwine, the house continues
to reflect the warm devotion of its owning
family as home to D'Arcy Wyvill – who
took over the property from his parents
Charlie and Maggie in 2017 – his wife
Imogen and their three children.

Constable Burton Hall was designed
by John Carr of York, one of the most
successful architects operating in

← The Palladian ideal: the entrance front of 1760s Constable Burton Hall, designed by architect John Carr of York and inspired by Palladio's Villa Emo.

eighteenth-century Yorkshire.[2] A notable local figure, he was twice Lord Mayor of York and acquired his own country estate. The fifth volume of *Vitruvius Britannicus* by John Woolfe and James Gandon (1771) contains more plates of architecture by Carr (including Constable Burton Hall) than by any other single architect, exceeding even those dedicated to Robert Adam. All the leading London architects, including Adam and Sir William Chambers, were members of the Surveyors' Club; Carr was the only non-London architect to be invited to become an honorary member, a place he took up in 1791.

Carr bridged the Palladian, rococo and neoclassical with earnest good practice and 'good taste';[3] his greatest project was probably Harewood House in Yorkshire, built in 1759–71 for the Lascelles family.[4] Wisely, he made annual visits to London, which gave him enough of the air of a designer of fashion to satisfy many Yorkshire gentlemen and others beyond the county borders. Giles Worsley has written of his work: 'never showy, always verging on the side of restraint, his buildings show an effortless ability to develop and vary a classical theme'.[5] It is a description that characterises the interiors of Constable Burton.

Carr's carefully judged and modelled house for Sir Marmaduke Wyvill, 7th Baronet, was inspired by one of Andrea Palladio's most assured and compact designs, the Villa Emo, near Fanzolo, in the Veneto, Italy. To this, Carr added an additional storey while omitting the balancing wings.[6] The Villa Emo has a central recessed portico under a triangular pediment on the entrance elevation, and long arcaded wings stretching out

to pavilions.[7] Palladio published his elevations and plans in *I Quattro Libri*, in 1570, and this handy reference work was much reproduced in the early eighteenth century. Carr may have turned to a set of reproductions in Isaac Ware's *The Four Books of Andrea Palladio's Architecture* (1738).[8]

While rooted in the Palladian tradition, the sculptural simplicity of the 1760s house has a pared-down quality that seems to connect with more forward-looking neoclassical taste. It replaced an Elizabethan manor of considerable extent that stood on the site, one which is recorded along with its elaborate formal gardens in an engraving by Johannes Kip in *Britannia Illustrata* (1707–9). The artist Joseph Farington related a story allegedly told to Lord Muncaster by the Reverend Charles Wyvill (Sir Marmaduke's successor), that this older house was pulled down by Carr of York's workmen entirely by accident, 'and this mistake, as Carr called it, cost Sir Marmaduke £10,000 to build another house'.[9] However, the idea that Sir Marmaduke would have retained his architect under these circumstances stretches the story beyond credulity.

Carr created a five-bay-by-seven-bay house of fine smooth ashlar, with the entrance front to the west. The recessed three-bay, first-floor portico of Ionic columns fills two storeys above the rusticated basement, with boldly detailed windows – the latter almost echoing works by Sir John Vanbrugh; as at Emo, this recessed portico sits under a triangular pediment. The main reception rooms run along the seven-bay south front, which is composed of two bays on either side of a slightly projecting central three; these

→→ Tall mirrors against the intense blue of the walls enhance the height and light of the drawing room.

are also crowned with a triangular pediment. The east face is broken by a central full-height bay window that serves the dining room on the *piano nobile* and the bedroom above.

The fluent plan of the *piano nobile* is typical of the socially inflected house planning of the mid-eighteenth century, something that also works surprisingly

well in the twenty-first. The well-lit entrance hall, known as the outer hall, catches the sun through the portico and forms a kind of open loggia from which to view the evening sunset. South of the hall lies the library-come-billiard room, and the entrance hall leads to the staircase hall (the inner hall), a dramatic room rising the full height of the house, top lit from

↑ The dining room, looking towards the staircase hall and entrance hall: the warm cream, browns and pinks are all based on analysis of the historic interior schemes. The elegant Gillow furniture was made originally for another family home, Denton Park.

demi-lunette windows. There is a cantile-vered stone staircase with wrought-iron balustrade, and both outer and inner rooms have stone-flagged floors. The walls of the inner hall provide a hang-ing space for the largest pictures of the house, and the room acts as a pivot to the plan, giving access to both the drawing room and dining room.

From the 1970s, the Wyvill family have carried out a long programme of redeco-ration with advice from furniture expert Patrick Dingwall and from Nigel Leaney, a paint expert and specialist in John Carr of York interiors. The latter's guidance on colours and paints has resulted in both the peacock blue of the drawing room, and the dark cream, brown and red of

↑ The dining room table, with the handsome 1760s marble chimneypiece behind, is laid for the entertainment of a shooting party.

the dining room. In 2016 the outer hall was redecorated in stone colours and refurnished in the manner of a 'living hall' with piano and chair; Imogen Wyvill sees it as a place where you can enjoy the view, observing that 'the light in this room is very special'.[10] D'Arcy has also commissioned new pieces of furniture made from Constable Burton oak by Sam Anderson; these reflect his belief in the idea that 'it's important that each generation adds something for the future'.

The best pictures and Gillow-made furniture came from another family estate, Denton Park in Yorkshire, also built by Carr of York (and described by John Britton as 'superbly furnished' in 1812[11]). The two estates were united after 1861 and for several decades the Wyvill family lived principally at Denton Park, before returning to Constable Burton Hall in 1901.[12] Several of the Gillow items were modelled on Thomas Chippendale's *The Gentleman and Cabinet-Maker's Director* (1754); despite a sale in 1932, many fine pieces remain in the family, and can be seen especially in the dining room. Threads of history play an important role in the interiors, and from Denton Park came Philip Mercier portraits of the Ibbotsons and Grand Tour views now hanging in the drawing room at Constable Burton Hall. Portraits of Sir Marmaduke and his wife Henrietta are also in the drawing room, while there is a portrait by Andrew Festing of Charles Wyvill as High Sheriff of North Yorkshire (in 1986–87) in the dining room.

Charlie and Maggie Wyvill oversaw a major refurbishment of the house in the 1970s, after the house had been tenanted for a time. Determined to bring it back into family occupation, they made Constable Burton Hall famous as a destination for shooting parties for international clients. This side of the estate business continues today under D'Arcy's management, while his parents still live on the estate.

The setting of Constable Burton Hall is part of the essential character of the house, contributing spectacular views and filtering in the light that animates the principal rooms and bedrooms. Allées and rides cut through the surrounding woods give more distant views of unexpected drama, and a tall lime avenue links the house to the still productive kitchen gardens in an especially cherished part of the estate. Here, reflective ponds retain the association of a historic icehouse and a memorable water garden has been planted around the stream. Further on is a remarkable and atmospheric wooded valley known as the Deene. A terraced woodland garden of lilies, ferns and hardy shrubs is thought to echo some of the terraces created in the seventeenth century; these were softened in the 1920s and '30s by then tenant Mrs Burdon who planted roses and wildflowers. A dream for future fulfilment is research into the original eighteenth-century pleasure gardens.

Constable Burton Hall represents the strand of English country-house building that is part of the tapestry of English life. A mid-Georgian house in a landscaped park, it is still the centre of a working estate and still home to the family that built it. Its interiors are linked on a social circuit devoted to the comfort of guests and informed by accumulated historical understanding. Its gardens are profuse but also artfully blended with nature.

→ *clockwise from top left:* a detail of the chimneypiece in the library; a detail of the upper level of the main top-lit staircase; eighteenth-century relief miniatures in the drawing room; the mid-eighteenth-century staircase, set up for entertainment.

PITSHILL

Classical dream reborn

GLORIOUSLY SITED, WITH OBLIQUE views south towards the Downs, not far from Petworth in Sussex, stands Pitshill, a glowing, seven-bay classical, pedimented house in a green and shaded combe. Today, this speaks both about the beauty of neoclassical architecture in the English landscape and about the determination, skills and taste that it takes to revive such beauty. The Hon. Charles Pearson and his wife Lila have carried out a magnificent revival, which they began planning in the late 1990s.[1] The renewed house might well be described as a work of art in its own right – a physical demonstration of the building and decorative skills in the high classical tradition that can still be called upon in the twenty-first century.

Despite its placid stillness in the vibrantly green landscape, Pitshill has a surprisingly complex history. One William Mitford had acquired the estate in 1760, and his son, also William, subsequently sought to remodel the original gabled, stone Jacobean house (depicted in a drawing by Samuel Hieronymous Grimm) with a projecting two-storeyed porch similar to that at nearby Manor of Dean.[2] In the end Mitford replaced it with the magnificent neoclassical house that we see today. It is a matter of some debate how the design evolved. Mitford first looked to the architect Sir John Soane, but in the end it seems he rejected Soane's scheme, which would have formed a grand addition linked to the original house, and decided to build anew.[3]

The final design may well have been his own, but was evidently inspired by Soane's elegant vision. Mitford was

assisted by John Upton, the capable surveyor to the Petworth estate, in West Sussex. There was some further elaboration of the house in the 1830s, especially to the interiors, but also included such things as the addition of a glazed veranda on the south face. In the 1950s the attic floor was removed, as were accretions to the north.

Charles Pearson, second son of the 3rd Viscount Cowdray, grew up at nearby Cowdray Park, and knows this area of Sussex exceptionally well. Indeed, he visited Pitshill from early childhood and recollects: 'I was at school with Edwin, the youngest son of Sir Colville and Lady Barclay, who had bought it in the Fifties. I think I was captivated by it even then'.[4] He explored the house and grounds as a child and went to some of his first dances in the house as a teenager. Its magic remained with him.

The Pearsons bought Pitshill in 1997 but had not anticipated that it would take so much time to prepare the site (which included rerouting and improving a public footpath). Charles recalls: 'The house was much loved but in a poor state when we bought it – isolated and pale, with a backdrop of holm oaks'.[5] The extensive restoration work on the house and garden did not really begin until 2010 and was finished in 2016; in 2017 it won a well-deserved Georgian Group award.

Christopher Smallwood, the architect who had been working on the new family entrance at Goodwood House, also in West Sussex, was appointed and helped the Pearsons give Pitshill back some of its missing features. Smallwood designed a portico for the restored original western entrance, with paired and fluted Portland stone Doric columns. The central staircase hall has been improved, and a secondary stair to the attic floor introduced within a new mansard roof containing extra bedrooms. Smallwood retired during the project, which ultimately passed to Giles Quarme.[6] Armands Balams, joiner, cabinetmaker and carver, led an outstanding team of Latvian craftsmen, and Edward Bulmer, the interior designer who worked on Althorp in Northamptonshire and Goodwood, has also played a major role in the final realisation of the interior character.

The house now rises with a crisp, formal elegance so entirely in the spirit of the late Georgian period it is hard to imagine the sheer scale of the renovations that had to be carried out, and which also render the house so elegant within. The work included the dismantling of the east façade, in order to clean the stone and restore it. Around 80 per cent of the original stone was preserved and cleaned while the rest was replaced; the other elevations were rendered to match the Portland stone. The original Coade stone balustrades and tympanum palmette decoration were also restored.

The interiors have been fully revived, decorated and furnished with a very clear vision around a carefully chosen date span of 1785 to 1835.[7] This became a key to the brief for colour, furnishing and textiles, on which Charles Pearson was advised by Bulmer, who produced detailed coloured drawings to help visualise the proposals for each room, and create a smooth and fluent sense of movement around the house.

The original plan flows well around the great top-lit staircase, with tall doors and rooms filled with light. On the principal

←← The damask-hung dining room is filled with fine portraits by Sir Thomas Lawrence and Sir Joshua Reynolds from the Pearsons' former Aberdeenshire home.

ground floor, there is the entrance hall, the coolly classical staircase hall and garden hall, the drawing room, dining room, breakfast room, morning room and study. The drawing room with its soft grey walls is closely hung with a fine collection of French Arcadian landscape and ruin views, and has a splendid carpet copied from a French Napoleonic original, woven by David Bamford

of Presteigne, with the Pearson crest included in the corners; the curtains are a Clermont fabric called 'Milton'.[8]

The red-damask dining room is hung with portraits by Sir Thomas Lawrence and Sir Joshua Reynolds from the Pearsons' former Aberdeenshire house. The dining room has another Bamford-woven carpet, this one based on an early nineteenth-century original from Dudmaston in

↑ The morning room has the perfect combination: comfortable seating and late eighteenth-century paintings.

Shropshire, and the curtains are a cut-velvet damask from Watts & Co. The carpet in the morning room was copied from an example at Hinton Ampner in Hampshire with the ground colours changed, and the curtains a chintz from Colefax and Fowler. The curtains have all been made up by Ian Block of A.T. Cronin, and the curtain boxes were designed by Bulmer, with trimmings by Haywards.

The restoration of the top-lit staircase hall, which had been altered in the 1950s, was, as Charles Pearson says himself, 'the crowning glory of the house'.9 A new domed Soanian-style ceiling was designed by Giles Quarme and Archie Walls as the final interior triumph (with fine decorative work by Stephen Pettifer). Bulmer puts the greatest emphasis on 'sorting out a house for people to live in

comfortably, while respecting the original architecture' and stresses the rigour of his clients in having such a clear vision of the result.[10]

The Arcadian character of the house is enhanced throughout by well-chosen landscape paintings, which echo the memorable views from the windows. Among those acquired especially for the revived interiors of Pitshill is the giant-size Anton Hallmann depiction of the Villa Medici that hangs in the staircase hall, and three works by Robert Adam's favoured decorative painter, the talented Antonio Zucchi, originally painted for Adam's entrance hall at Compton Verney in Warwickshire. Bulmer prepared designs for new frames following the model of the Adam-designed plaster frames based on the Compton Verney originals, which were

then carved in wood by Julian Stanley and gilded by Simon Cooper.

There have been many skilled crafts-men involved, and they are a roll call of the best in their respective fields. Jerry Rothman provided specialist cabinetmak-ing and carving; the wallpapers in the house are by David Skinner and Hamilton Weston; the painting, gilding and marbling are by Hesp Jones & Co.; and the plaster-work is by Stevensons of Norwich.[11] The new oak floors are by Weldon, and David Wilkinson supplied much of the lighting. The electrified picture rails meant that there was no need to chase additional wir-ing into the historic walls to provide subtle and adjustable lighting.

A handsome new formal garden has been laid out to designs by Simon Johnson, with a generously wide lawn and

← The extraordinary quality and attention to detail of this restoration project is revealed in the tassels, fringes and drops of the curtains throughout the principal rooms. The curtains are made up by Ian Block of A.T. Cronin.

↑ A neoclassical drapery style for the curtains in the drawing room, designed by Edward Bulmer.

← The study has some of the best views in the house, looking across the remarkable landscape in which Pitshill sits.

swimming pool and pedimented Tuscan-style temple-like pool pavilion; the whole merges gently with wonderful views. The lawn is framed by clipped holm oaks. Philip Thomason supplied Coade stone balustrading for both the house and for the lion-mask fountain north of the pavilion. This formal area close to the house fades into traditional English parkland and then merges into the wider landscape beyond. The ha-ha wall was reconstructed, and an original shell house, which terminates a terrace walk, was restored.

It must be said that the sheer quality and finish of architecture, interiors and gardens at Pitshill is remarkable. The revived and much-loved house seems almost to float in its Sussex landscape setting. It must be acknowledged as a living celebration of late Georgian neo-classical taste, in which the conservation and restoration work has given this house all the qualities of the perfect country house, for living, entertaining and enjoying the indoor and outdoor pleasures of country life.

↑ The extensive formal gardens designed by Simon Johnson underscore Pitshill's idyllic setting.

CHYKNELL HALL

Regency elegance reborn

CHYKNELL HALL IN SHROPSHIRE has the reserved, classical, lightly Italianate quality of the Regency country house. Houses of this period are a kind of high point of English domestic design, with their eminently liveable and compact plans; cool, elegant exteriors; and their strong sense of connection to the joys of the garden and the sporting pleasures of the country estate more widely. The feel of the house itself is similar to that associated with the work of John Nash, but in this case it is the work of John Haycock of Shrewsbury, who designed many important public and private buildings in Shropshire and Montgomeryshire.

The estate was acquired in 2015 by Princess Corinna zu Sayn-Wittgenstein-Sayn, who has overseen a major restoration with her son Prince Alexander zu Sayn-Wittgenstein-Sayn, in which the interior designer, Guy Goodfellow of London, has played a major role.[1] The ambition has been to realise the inherent character of this comfortable, classical Regency house, both for family occupation and for entertaining, and to modernise it while respecting its history.

Chyknell Hall is well documented, and the papers at Chyknell have recently been catalogued by Michael Tollemache.[2] There was an older house on the site that had belonged to the Potter and Farmer families, and this appears to have been partly absorbed into its Regency successor. One Sarah Farmer married John Taylor, 'ironmonger of Wolverhampton', in 1736, and their son Edward Farmer Taylor, born in 1740, was evidently set up for a comfortable life. John Taylor died in 1746,

and his widow Sarah managed the estate until their son came of age and beyond.

Edward Farmer Taylor, who was a canny businessman with interests in the City of London, added to the estate and built a substantial brick stable yard at Chyknell in around 1792. Taylor's grandson, christened Frederick but known simply as 'Farmer' Taylor, inherited the estate in 1811. He lived the life of a sociable country gentleman, staying often at Hawarden Castle in Flintshire.

Farmer Taylor invited architect John Haycock to redesign the main house. Local historian William Dawkes referenced a now-lost diary of Farmer Taylor and noted that in February 1813, 'four men were employed at Chyknell, in throwing up clay, preparatory to making bricks intended for the new house at Chyknell which was finally completed and occupied in 1817'.[3]

Two of Haycock's 1814 plans survive in the house and both show the 'Old House' in light grey wash as retained. One of these proposals was for a far grander property, anticipating his marriage, with Haycock proposing, in effect, a U-shape plan.[4] A new entrance front of six bays was to be created with two setback side wings, one being the old house, the wings being screened by colonnades, and the main front divided by a staircase with grand reception rooms either side. The improvements were clearly much modified in execution, with a considerably more restrained but still elegant staircase and with a good dining room and drawing room, but both of these now face east.

The walls were of brick and rendered, the roof was of slate and the tall ground-floor sash windows invited connection with the gardens. Farmer Taylor was keen to establish himself in the county elite, and was highly successful in doing this: he was appointed High Sheriff of the county in 1815, and in 1816 married the Hon. Juliana Cavendish, daughter of the 2nd Baron

Waterpark. The marriage settlement specifically references 'that newly erected mansion house ... and all that the old house or mansion with the Barns stables outhouses coachhouses'.[5] They had four sons, three of whom lived to adulthood, and in 1852 their son Henry Taylor inherited Chyknell.

In 1858 Henry (who adopted his mother's surname of Cavendish) commissioned Edward Haycock, son of John, to add a vast new dining room (which appears to have also doubled as a ballroom), which was executed during that year, along with some modifications to the service quarters. Haycock Jr's architectural plans remain in the house as well as estimates from the builder, John

Hand, and Thomas and John Groves; notes reference 'the new Portland cement' for the exterior, and the colours used, 'Bed rooms all white & light stone colour/Hall window shutters 2 shades of stone colour ... drawing rooms with paper'.[6] In 1862 Henry Cavendish was married to an heiress, Selina Gage, a granddaughter of 4th Viscount Gage, and they had four daughters, three of whom survived to adulthood.

In 1893 Henry and Selina's eldest daughter, Edith Selina, married Colonel Hubert Cornwall-Legh of High Legh Hall, Cheshire. With her sisters, she inherited a third share in the Chyknell estate in 1901; she lived the longest, whereby the property came to be hers. In 1949 the house and estate were then inherited by her cousin,

↑ The elegant entrance hall looks through the top-lit staircase. The screen of fluted Ionic columns was recently decorated to resemble scagliola.

↓ Pale-blue wool curtains, draped and hung in the Regency manner, add to both the elegance and warmth of the drawing room.

Major Edward Gage. Major Gage and his wife Thalia commissioned designs from the architect Trenwith Wills, who in the 1930s had been in partnership with Lord Gerry Wellesley (who became the 7th Duke of Wellington in 1943) and had worked on many major London and country houses, such as Hinton Ampner in Hampshire.

Wills carried out various alterations to the house, which included converting the 1850s dining room into a handsome library. The Gages also employed designer Russell Page to create formal gardens at Chyknell, which still provide the setting for the house today. Between 1968 and 2011, Chyknell was the home of Simon and Mary Kenyon-Slaney and their family – Simon being High Sheriff in 1980, as Major Gage had been in 1963.

In 2015 the estate was acquired by Princess Corinna zu Sayn-Wittgenstein-Sayn, who oversaw a major restoration and refurbishment of the house between July and December 2016, which included the renewal of the pale stone-coloured render of the exterior. Much emphasis has been laid on understanding the earlier history of the house, in which Michael Tollemache's researches have been of great use. Princess Corinna observes: 'We lived here for a year before we did anything, trying to understand how the house worked, and would work for us. We then approached Guy'.[7]

Guy Goodfellow trained as an architect and gained invaluable early experience over eight years at Colefax and Fowler where he became a design director. He went on to work on the restoration of

↑ The drawing room takes its warm-brown
wall colour from the large sketch of a hunting
tapestry on the wall at left, from Julia Boston
Antiques.

↑ A novel idea: upholstered corner seats are
designed for comfort and conversation.

a number of architecturally important houses, such as West Wycombe Park in Buckinghamshire for both the Dashwood family and the National Trust; Hopetoun House near Edinburgh, Scotland, for the Earl and Countess of Hopetoun; and Rosebery House, also near Edinburgh, for Lord and Lady Dalmeny. Goodfellow says, 'the joy of the country-house interior is to be found in the layering of textures, furniture, objects and art that have come together over time. I feel we have achieved this at Chyknell. My clients had a very clear vision that this should be a house for entertaining on a big scale but should also be comfortable and intimate for when the family is alone. We have managed to create a variety of exciting interior and exterior spaces that come into play at different times of the day, making weekend entertaining a pleasure. Among other things, I felt it was

important to create a more monumental feeling in the entrance hall, so I designed a chimneypiece and overmantel in the Palladian manner'.[8] This combines to give the room a feeling of quiet dignity and warmth. The walls have been painted in shades of grey and white, and the existing Ionic columns that divide the entrance from the staircase hall have been given a scagliola treatment by expert painter Piero Centofanti. A number of key pieces of antique furniture acquired especially for the house have come from Guinevere Antiques in London.

Princess Corinna says: 'Guy has a great eye and we like a sophisticated but understated look, and he helped us find solutions and antique furniture and paintings for the house. We would choose elements and then work out the decorative schemes around them. For instance, in the drawing room we first chose a large

↑ The Cinema Room is boldly designed with its lacquered blue panelling and James Bond posters.

→ The wall treatment in the dining room is a modern print on linen of a historic tapestry from Dumfries House in Scotland. This solution is both elegant and acoustically effective.

tapestry cartoon of a deer-hunting scene, from Julia Boston, and then built our colour scheme around the colours from that'.[9] The walls are a pale tobacco colour, the perfect backdrop for the carved marble chimneypiece, the eighteenth-century capriccio views of classical architectural scenes, and a huge portrait of an ancestor of Prince Alexander's who fought against Napoleon Bonaparte. The drawing room also has a large bay window overlooking the garden; elegant wool drapes perfectly capture the style of the period.

Seating throughout is comfortable and usable, and in this room and in the library there are upholstered corner seats that are a favoured feature for quiet conversation. In the drawing room a huge Ottoman is piled with books, suggesting the pleasures of a long weekend party. In the dining room a Zardi & Zardi reproduction of a tapestry of *The Triumph of Bacchus* from Dumfries House in Ayrshire, Scotland, printed on linen, has been introduced, which creates a fine backdrop to a well-laid dining table. The overmantel mirror is in white and gold and of Palladian character.

Goodfellow says: 'An important room is the library, originally a dining room, first fitted out as a library in 1949–50 in neoclassical style, but we have given it an additional richness'. The walls are papered in a restful green from the Guy Goodfellow range, and sofa covers are in a green chintz pattern from Jasper. Goodfellow recalls: 'as John Fowler said, "Greens always go with greens – just look at the hedgerows"'. The Egyptian Revival chimneypiece and white and gold overmantel neoclassical mirror were moved into this room from the hall.[10]

The television is screened by an estate map in the shelving when not in use, and subtle reading lights are provided throughout the room. Eighteenth- and nineteenth-century hound paintings hung around the chimneypiece complete the ensemble, a light-hearted contrast to the classical busts above the bookcases. A private cinema made comfortable with sofas is panelled in eighteenth-century style and lacquered in a deep blue. The classic James Bond movie posters add a final touch.

Bedrooms are comfortable and light. The master bedroom has a handsome posterbed and Bennison floral wallpaper; another suite is hung with a paper by Nicholas Haslam Ltd. Portraits of the Farmer Taylor family, who built and extended the early nineteenth-century house, remain in the collection and hang in the principal bedrooms.

The kitchen has been extended into the courtyard to give it extra depth for an integrated breakfast room. This room now opens out onto a courtyard in which Julian and Isabel Bannerman have added deft grotto-like touches.

One of the beauties of Chyknell Hall is its magnificent location, on a sheltered corner of a hill with surrounding woods and an extensive series of ponds, creating a landscape of the type that Humphry Repton might have suggested. It has a settled feel and has been lived in by only four families since the early 1800s. Its most recent restoration, well informed by historical understanding as much as aesthetic considerations, has judiciously enhanced its classic Regency country-house character. The natural colours and organic floral patterns underline an overall feeling of country comfort and elegance.

→ The handsome bed in the master bedroom stands against a Bennison floral wallpaper.

ON
FURNITURE

From the days of the great late seventeenth-century Stuart upholsterers to the fashionable 'shabby chic' of the 1970s, and on to the highly individual approaches explored in this book, furniture has helped English country houses communicate their qualities of charm, sophistication or prestige. Furniture is intrinsic to creating an atmosphere of comfort and convenience, and one of the joys of visiting an English country house is seeing the way in which furnishings are composed within rooms to form a living picture. From grand cabinets to textiles and paintings, they illuminate stories of family, connections, travel and changing taste. They are the pages in the book of the life of a house.

In historic houses we may marvel at how long an antique piece has been in the room it occupies today, but for much of history, furniture has been essentially a movable feature. Up until at least the sixteenth century, it was regarded as something that could be packed up and taken with the household when it travelled to other residences.[1] 'Movables' later became associated with those items that could be willed away from the house, unlike heirlooms – most often portraits – which would pass with the main house and estate. It is rare to find Tudor and early Stuart furniture still in its original houses (Hardwick Hall, Derbyshire, is a rare exception with some original Elizabethan furnishing in situ),[2] but from the nineteenth century, and especially in the early to mid-twentieth century, such pieces were frequently bought in

→ A George Bullock chair in neoclassical spirit
at Smedmore House, in Dorset, was originally in
the home of Emperor Napoleon when in exile on
St Helena, and later presented to a member of the
Mansel family who served in the garrison there.

by the owners of historic houses who scoured antique shops and auctioneers so they could furnish their interiors appropriately. At Haddon Hall, in the 1920s, the Duke of Rutland wanted furniture that would suit the rooms not only in period terms but also in relation to the atmosphere they evoked, a desire inspired by the contemporary admiration for Dutch seventeenth-century paintings of interiors.

Furniture is part of those 'conveniences and elegancies of polite life' so clearly admired by Washington Irving in his early nineteenth-century observations on the English country house in *The Sketchbook of Geoffrey Crayon Gent.* (1819).[3] As far back as Tudor times, country-house interiors were richly furnished. William Harrison's 1577 'Description of England' reveals that 'in nobleman's houses it is not rare to see an abundance of arras, rich hangings of tapestry, silver vessel, and so much other plate as may furnish sundry cupboards'.[4] His words evoke the light, colour and glamour that tapestries, hangings and silver brought to panelled rooms. This warmth and luxury would be enhanced by solid oak tables and chests, and these would also be covered in bright textiles and Turkey carpet. Often their patterns and decorations were drawn from engravings published in France, the Low Countries and Italy, by Jacques Androuet DuCerceau, Hans Vredeman de Vries and Sebastiano Serlio.[5]

In the late seventeenth century, skilled cabinetmakers produced sophisticated pieces that used the texture and colour of the wood itself as part of the decoration.[6] The range of woods included walnut, cherry, cedar, yew and olive, and inlaid marquetry was highly prized, as was the 'Japanned' cabinet, lacquered with gold ornamentation on a darker background. Upholstered furniture developed rapidly, finding its fullest voice in the state beds of the late seventeenth century with their lavish testers and hangings in silk.[7] The English country-house owner was a beneficiary of Louis XIV's 'Revocation of the Edict of Nantes' in 1685, which ended toleration of Protestantism in France and resulted in Huguenot (Protestant) craftsmen bringing their expertise from France to Britain, such as skilled designer-makers Daniel Marot and Francis Lapierre.[8] This was perhaps the great age of luxurious and expensive furniture,[9] and grand interiors remained rich with colour, texture and the exotic (imports from India, China and Japan). During a visit to Burghley House at the end of the seventeenth century, traveller Celia Fiennes made note of the 'tapestry all blew Silke and Rich gold thread': the perfect accompaniment to painted ceilings and Italian and French paintings.[10]

In the early Georgian period, furniture took on a more architectural character, associated with the fashion for Palladian interiors. Mahogany, imported from the

West Indies, became the most popular wood for elegant fittings and furnishings, and William Kent designed both stately mahogany pieces and ornate gilded pier tables and glasses.[11] London cabinetmakers began to dominate the national scene and one in particular, Thomas Chippendale, laid down a remarkable book of designs, *The Gentleman and Cabinet-Maker's Director* (1754). He stressed the relationship between cabinetmaking and architecture, the former being 'the most useful and ornamental' of the allied arts. This was illustrated in the book's engraved plates, accompanied by descriptions of the popular furniture of the day, including rococo ornament and nods to the styles of France, to Chinese and the Gothic.[12] Robert Adam encouraged an integrated and refined fashion in decoration that went on to influence furniture, leading Horace Walpole to quip archly: 'from Kent's mahogany we are dwindled to Adam's filigree'.[13]

Neoclassical architecture sat quite happily alongside ornate furniture in the mid-eighteenth century, but within interiors peppered with classical statuary and busts, and paintings of Italian landscapes. There was a gradual shift to more austere forms, rooted in classical models. Furniture of the early nineteenth century is characterised by darker woods, and their forms influenced by the ideal of Greek architecture illustrated in Thomas Hope's *Household Furniture and Interior Decoration* (1807), which also showed Egyptian and Indian styles.[14] Later Regency taste again embraced the glamour of France, and by the 1830s, furniture (as well as architecture) was being produced in a bewildering variety of styles: 'Grecian, Gothic or perpendicular, Elizabethan or Louis XIV'.[15]

A.W.N. Pugin was a champion of Gothic forms, and from the 1860s, this shift in imagery helped shape the principled Arts and Crafts reaction against mass manufacture. This gradually moved from its Gothic inspiration to simple, vernacular furniture, which might be seventeenth or eighteenth century in character and which paralleled the Aesthetic Movement interest in Japanese design and the 'artistic' interior, both tastes reflecting the idealisation of 'The House Beautiful'.[16]

Between the 1890s and 1930s, country-house furnishing was influenced rather less by new design and more by refined and aestheticised versions of period styles. This can be seen in the frozen black-and-white interiors that appeared in *Country Life* during these years, reflecting a trend that continued into the 1950s.[17] Well-chosen antiques were the popular mode for drawing rooms and dining rooms, with Jacobean or older pieces mixed with choice examples from the late seventeenth century. The atmosphere of Haddon Hall and Beckley Park evoke this era today, combined with modern touches, echoing the phrase Juliette Huxley used to describe Garsington Manor in Oxfordshire while the home of Philip and Lady Ottoline Morrell: namely a 'habitable work of art'.[18] In 1909 architect Henry Shapland wrote *Style Schemes in Antique Furnishings*, in which he sought to show 'how the right appreciation of tradition will prevent making a living-room a species of modern museum, or a more heterogeneous collection of furniture and bric-à-brac, thrown together in a haphazard way'.[19]

By the 1930s, increasing interest in the Georgian period had changed approaches to furnishing, and the arrangement of pieces was governed by symmetry and convenience. When compared to similar views from the early 1900s, *Country Life* pictures in these years show rooms becoming more sparsely furnished, eschewing the perhaps overblown comfort embodied in late Victorian and Edwardian ideals.[20] Rooms were laid out with elegance in mind, with space left around items of furniture so that line and colour could be more fully enjoyed. This is exemplified in the interiors of Kelmarsh Hall, Northamptonshire, when it was occupied by Nancy Lancaster (then Mrs Ronald Tree).[21] Caroline Seebohm reflected on her childhood homes to summon up the typical country-house interior of mid-century England: 'My parents' taste for chintz upholstery, Georgian furniture, Persian carpets, and watercolor paintings done by our relatives, was as timeless as the grandfather clock in the hall'.[22] But this style of 'timeless' Englishness was a distinctly twentieth-century one, the result of an amalgam of inherited flavours and ideals.

The Second World War produced a fundamental change. In the 1950s Fowler and other designers encouraged country-house owners to use the furniture they had around them to make comfortable and elegant interiors that would work in properties with smaller numbers of domestic staff.[23] It was a composed and clever approach that, in turn, influenced the famous 'shabby chic' of the 1970s and '80s.[24] Antique collecting hit a new high and the 'country-house look' (as discussed in the introduction) began to influence styles in the town house and even spread across the world; the ideal was a touch of warm colour, old pieces of furniture supported by comfortable, well-upholstered sofas and chairs, and connections to the garden echoed in floral patterns and chintz. As influential interior designer David Mlinaric observed in *Mlinaric on Decorating* (2008), 'large historic houses ... seemed to have no role, but were anachronisms, impossible and burdensome ... But this has changed into an appreciation of their historical interest and beauty'.[25]

In the early 2000s a less dogmatic 'cool' contemporary design began to dilute this look in town. Within the country house, however, the presence of antique furniture and an emphasis on comfort and upholstery has kept something of that look, although often manifested in different ways. It is, in the end, always a balance between style and patterns of living, and in this book we can see collections that have been assembled and blended with inherited pieces and portraits (for instance, at Sezincote, Pitshill and Chyknell). Other interiors have been put together with a more individualistic or artistic approach, such as those at Voewood and Walcot. Vann reflects an Arts and Crafts layering of new and old, while Eastridge is a new house that combines traditional and modern in a spirit of light and comfort. Many of the houses in this book have either recently undergone a generational change, or have been restored and furnished by new owners, allowing us to see how each owner and generation brings their touch and vision to the enterprise. Furnishing the country house remains a very personal pursuit, tailored and flavoured to those who live there.

→ Looking from the morning room into the long drawing room of Wolverton Hall, Worcestershire, a bookish paradise owned by two writers.

WOLVERTON HALL

A country place for writing

IT IS TEMPTING TO SEE WOLVERTON Hall, in Worcestershire, as something of a writers' retreat, as it is the house where Nicholas Coleridge has penned several of his novels. His wife Georgia, a professional healer and therapist, has also written a number of books on the healing arts here at Wolverton. The dining room is lined with colourfully bound volumes of the magazines of the London branch of the Condé Nast Group, of which Nicholas was chairman for thirty years – he is one of the greatest modern champions of the printed page.

Georgia 'writes in a space between our bedroom and the bathroom', while Nicholas usually writes in the garden, in the open air, enjoying the serene privacy that can only be found in the shade of a classic English red-brick 'Queen Anne'

house.[1] They also recently (in 2019) completed a new two-storey brick folly, an octagonal tower in a walled garden in the 'Gothick' spirit, designed by classical master Quinlan Terry, which, in effect, has another writing room on its first floor, and a summer dining room on the ground floor. The top is a platform for drinks in the summer under the stars.[2]

The Coleridges acquired Wolverton Hall in 2004, and have made it a much-loved home for their family of four children, surrounded by the usual accoutrements of walled gardens, barns and coach house (now a staff cottage). They revel in the history of the house and site, and are conscious of how the house has been shaped and adapted throughout this time. Nicholas Coleridge says: 'we did a lot of work when we bought it, and every

eighteen months a different room or area has been given additional attention'.[3]

Nicholas Coleridge grew up near Midhurst in Sussex and loved country life, but his work has mostly been London-based; he had always dreamed of a restoration project of such a house as this one. He and Georgia have both enjoyed the renovation and revival of Wolverton Hall: making the circuit of rooms work and bringing into them a new feeling of light, colour, warmth and comfort has been a rewarding experience. A warren of well-appointed bedrooms and bathrooms speaks of the couple's innate sociability. He says: 'it has been a very good focus for family life, and the perfect party house; while it works well for us when we are alone, the Victorian wing means that we have enough bedrooms to put up a good number of friends – or more often the friends of our children – which we especially enjoy'.[4] To this end

the barn was also adapted so it could, on occasion, be used as a 'party barn'.

Wolverton Hall was built around 1709 for the Actons, a family of recusant land-owners, on the site of a sixteenth-century manor house of which little is known.[5] The design of the new folly has been informed by the imagined architecture of this manor house. Georgia Coleridge observes: 'Quinlan Terry wanted the folly to feel like it might have been here before the main house was built'.

The south front of the house has seven bays and the east side has six. On the east side is an off-centre doorcase with a segmental pediment, leading to the garden, and the main entrance is on the west side with a Tuscan order porch, thought to be from the early twentieth century.[6] The house is built in brick, which while essentially uniform varies in colour from a rose pink to a plum colour, with stone quoins, while the slated roof is mostly concealed

by a brick parapet. To the south-west lies the five-bay brick coach house with a hipped roof, dated 1714, and behind this is a barn, part sixteenth century and part nineteenth century, and a timber-framed hen house, which also appears to be a sixteenth-century building.

The original entrance to the main house was in the central bay of the south front, the only front to have a stone platband and keystones in the rubbed-brick flat-arch voussoirs over the windows.[7] The present main entrance is approached through a courtyard framed by a nineteenth-century service wing. It seems that the relocating of the entrance hall was done in the early nineteenth century in order to turn the capacious and well-lit space into a south-facing draw-ing room, which remains today. One of the finest original elements of the house is the handsome staircase of the early 1700s – the walls are hung with large framed photographs of the Coleridges' various world travels, especially around India, and fashion shoots.

The house was built for a William Acton, who died in 1725. The Actons were an old Worcestershire family originally based at Ombersley but established at Wolverton from 1585, although nothing is known of the presumed Elizabethan house they occupied until the early 1700s. As Nicholas Kingsley observes, 'The Actons of Wolverton were a recusant family who followed the Catholic faith consistently through the 17th, 18th and 19th centuries; many of their daughters took the veil in convents in Belgium and France. Because of their faith, the men of the family were, until the 19th century, denied a University education and the public offices which their prominence

in the county would otherwise have delivered'.[8]

There were some modest additions in the mid-nineteenth century, mostly to extend the service accommodation. The house passed by descent in the Acton family into the twenty-first century. It was possibly William Joseph Acton, who inherited it in 1814 and married in 1833, who made the alterations to the entrance and dining room. An 1840 tithe map shows that the main part of the barn was built between 1840 and 1870. In 1840 there was a northwards extension from the older part of the barn (shown on some later maps, but it no longer exists), and there was a completely separate L-shaped building over what is now the entrance courtyard.

Wolverton Hall was leased out in the nineteenth century and lived in by Robert and Lady Catherine Berkeley in 1864–69, Robert being the heir to Spetchley Park in Worcestershire; in the 1880s it was leased by Sir Walter Greene, Master of Foxhounds of the Earl of Coventry's pack of hounds.[9] Another William Acton lived in the house in the mid-twentieth century and in the 1960s gave it to his daughter (Caroline) Lady Dawson, wife of Major Sir Trevor Dawson, 3rd Baronet. During the 1980s, the house passed through a few new owners before being bought by the Elliots, from whom the Coleridges acquired it.

The interiors of the house today have a relaxed and spacious sense of comfort and style. The south-facing drawing room is painted a pale primrose yellow, and fur-nished in soft pastel colours; the curtains are made from sailcloth from Ian Mankin in Fulham. The tall bookcases in this room, painted in a stone colour, and their

→ The dining room looking into the kitchen: issues of the magazines that owner Nicholas Coleridge oversaw as publisher are bound in multiple volumes, each with its own colour.

The bright and spacious family kitchen with its cheerful colours is fitted out in an Edwardian addition on the south-east side of the house.

echo of Indian tenting, were made up to a design by Hugh St Clair, friend and 'interiors guru', by cabinetmaker John Ives, who is based at Houghton in Norfolk. A fine portrait of an Indian maharajah from Bengal hangs in this room ('spotted for us thirty years ago by Philip Mould, he was apparently a playwright but his name has been lost to us').[10]

Books also fill one wall of the adjoining morning room, on the south-east corner of the house, which leads to the east-facing dining room. The panelled entrance hall, home to the piano, appears to have been remodelled in the mid-twentieth century, and links to the small room called 'the Drinks Room', where the cocktail cabinet is kept, and the décor of which is influenced 'by Robin Birley's club, 5 Hertford Street'.

The spacious and light family kitchen was laid out with advice from Hugh St Clair: plain units with slate tops (painted custard yellow and robin's egg blue) and a long table for family meals. This room fills the three-bay single-storey extension that seems to have been first added as a new dining room in the early 1900s, on the north-east corner of the house. Bedrooms are large and colourful, with bold floral wallpapers from Cole & Son and Colefax and Fowler. The striped wool stair runner on the main staircase was woven specially by Roger Oates, based nearby in Herefordshire.

Nicholas Coleridge says of his early morning writing sessions in the garden at Wolverton: 'I love those first three hours of the day, with the sun coming up over the oak trees and the dew evaporating from the lawn'.[11] Partly inspired by these early morning communications with house, garden and nature, he has planted many trees at Wolverton, including oaks, horse chestnuts and copper beech.

Sited in the walled former kitchen garden, which also houses the swimming pool, the new folly was inspired by many holidays in Landmark Trust properties, and Nicholas Coleridge recalls: 'Quinlan took us to see the banqueting house at Long Melford Hall, in Suffolk, but it turned out a little different, with an internal staircase, a kind of Tudor, Jacobean, Georgian amalgam'. The enclosed garden is now planted semi-formally with advice from the Oxfordshire-based garden designer James Alexander-Sinclair and Butter Wakefield.

One cannot help feeling that there is a novel yet to be written about a rather extraordinary episode in the life of Wolverton Hall, when it served as the stronghold of the van Moppe brothers. The brothers had spirited a stock of Dutch industrial diamonds into England just before German forces entered Amsterdam in May 1940.[12] The operation was overseen by Winston Churchill (then First Sea Lord), who understood the importance of denying the Nazi armaments industry use of essential commodities. At Wolverton the van Moppes were given bodyguards disguised as domestic servants.[13] Later in the war, the house was the headquarters of the Auxiliary Patrols in Worcestershire, who trained there in readiness to sabotage the anticipated German invasion, under the command of these same Dutch brothers, code-named 'Castor and Pollux'. Houses like Wolverton Hall always have as many hidden stories to be explored as there are rooms to be enjoyed.

→ The joy of the new: the two-storey octagonal 'Gothick' folly completed in 2019. Designed by architect Quinlan Terry, it contains a writing room and a summer dining room.

EASTRIDGE

The living expression of the classical

PART OF THE JOY OF SO MANY English country houses is the layered stories in which they are steeped: the distinctive and attractive form that comes from additions and contractions across centuries, and the underlying sense of how they are shaped by the lives led within them. Since the Regency, architects have designed houses that echo this narrative form, which imply history and reflect the aesthetic of these older houses. Edwin Lutyens was a master of such compositions, designing new houses that on one level feel like sketches of old organic houses, but with all the advantages of better building systems. Eastridge in Wiltshire, completed in 2018, is a contemporary demonstration of this same theme, resulting in a finely modelled house, a two-storey, five-bay classical block with low two-storey wings, mansard roofs and an additional eastern range that faces a walled garden.[1]

Eastridge was designed by Francis Terry, one of the leading younger classical architects in practice today.[2] According to Terry, 'The truth is we designed this house from the inside out; thinking about how life would be lived and the rooms that were needed, and then developed the best classical form for the exterior: life came first'.[3] Terry is well known for his draughtsmanship and for his skill in drawing out sketch elevations and plans by hand as they are discussed with clients – this is what happened at Eastridge.

He says, 'we wove a kind of narrative around the final form. I imagined a smart gentleman farmer building a simple early

↓ Completed in 2018, Eastridge, with its detailing, sash windows, smooth ashlar walls and symmetrical wings, combines eighteenth century and early twentieth-century ideals of classical elegance and fluid interior space.

Georgian box, and then James Wyatt–like wings being added by a Grand Tourist in the eighteenth century, and filled with Italian treasures and imported chimney-pieces, and then in the nineteenth century when times were harder, the wings were reduced. Later Lutyens appeared and gave the wings their cheerful French mansard roofs and added the rooms to the west with their Palladian-inspired windows looking across to the walled garden. The summer house was added in the 1960s by Oliver Messel'. It is a story told with self-deprecating humour and real affection for the house itself, which appealed deeply to his clients, Mr and Mrs Hambro, as they developed the project as a home for themselves and their three children.

In fact, the first part of the project to be realised was the summer house – part pool house, part retreat from the main house – which provided the arena for family recreation. It is a simple classical pavilion, with a portico with a shaped gable as a pediment – hence Terry's wry reference to Oliver Messel, the gifted theatre designer who turned to architectural

→ A view looking out to a sculpture by Sir Antony Gormley and the Wiltshire landscape beyond.

projects in the 1960s and '70s, especially in Barbados and Mustique.[4]

Within the summer house there is a generously scaled large family living room, with changing rooms and a place for al fresco meals in front. It is set in a new walled garden, of traditional vernacular build in brick and flint, and planted with borders on which the garden designer Rupert Golby advised. Golby is skilled in the subtle reinterpretation of the romantic classic English garden tradition with simpler planting and a sense of connection with the wider setting. The summer-house project provided something of a trial run for the main house, and much pleasure was achieved in the realisation of the union of architecture, garden and landscape.

The main house is also satisfyingly simple, and despite its plain, crisp ashlar walls, and the formal rhythm of its sash windows and pedimented dormers, it has a sculpted, slightly baroque feel in the way the shadow is cast between the connected blocks of the composition. There is a dignified, alert quality to the property, which owes much to the rigorous proportions of the house, windows and wings.

Eastridge is faced in a light, creamy Bath stone ashlar, under a slate roof, and set against a wooded backdrop; the south front looks out over a lake. It is the result of years of planning and careful design

↑ The entrance hall combines with the principal staircase of the house, and also forms a comfortable 'living hall'.

→ Cheerful curtains in shades of pink and brown in the breakfast room frame views across the garden.

and artisanship (Ketton Stone for the facing ashlar, R.W. Armstrong builders, joinery by S.B. Joinery and plasterwork by Stevensons of Norwich).

The Hambros had very strong ideas about how the house should work for family life and the kinds of rooms they wanted. This was inspired in part by former family homes, including Eastwell House in Kent and Dunley Manor in Hampshire. Mr Hambro, for instance, grew up at a house called Durrington, in Essex, a building of several periods with a strong Georgian element: a comfortable, modelled, mellow stuccoed house. Having such exemplars in mind helped

to prioritise certain arrangements and volumes within Eastridge, and those in turn dictated the exterior form, resulting in the almost sculpted composition that strikes the eye on the approach.

The contained quality of the exterior leads to a genuine sense of surprise inside: the house has generously scaled interiors, and tall sash windows flood the rooms with light. The main entrance hall is designed to link with a cross-axial corridor, the passage being indicated by a screen of columns, echoing the arrangements in eighteenth-century houses such as Dumfries House in Ayrshire, Scotland, behind which is an

↑ With its high ceiling and generous scale, the drawing room was inspired by favourite rooms in older family houses. Jane Ormsby Gore advised on interior colour, furnishings and fabrics.

↓ The summer house provides a splendid recreation space for the whole family in the summer months.

apsidal staircase compartment with a finely detailed oak staircase.

The well-proportioned drawing room and billiard room, separated by double doors, fill the south front, and have fine views across the wider landscape. The long dining room, kitchen and breakfast room are situated at the east end, with other supporting spaces, including a generous inner hall and boot room, that essential space of country-house life. The breakfast room is especially attractive, with a Venetian window facing east, to enjoy the morning sun. On the first floor a long, broad axial corridor links the bedrooms, and those in the wings are also more low-ceilinged, which gives them a homely feel.

The interiors are mellow and bright, with inherited furniture from other family homes, comfortable upholstered chairs and sofas, and Mr Hambro's extensive collection of mid-twentieth-century British art. Interior design advice was also provided by Jane Ormsby Gore, who grew up on the Welsh borders.[5] Her father, Lord Harlech, was ambassador to the US, so she lived for a while in the famous Lutyens-designed embassy there, and has a good understanding of classical interiors; she has worked on numerous country-house interiors, from Ashdown House in Berkshire to Chilham Castle in Kent.[6]

Throughout the rooms at Eastridge there is an emphasis on comfort, ease of circulation and appropriateness. Colours

are in an earthy natural range and pleasantly recessive, such as Naples Yellow, a primrose yellow and a soft moss green in principal rooms, where there are full curtains at the windows, and good-quality upholstered furniture with touches of Indian and Middle Eastern fabrics in the cushions.

Building a new house in the country is a particular challenge, but at Eastridge it was met with considerable thought, research and design imagination. The house forms not only a chapter in this book but a chapter in the continuing history of English classical country-house design in the twenty-first century.

Francis Terry is the son of renowned classical architect Quinlan Terry, designer of numerous admired neo-Palladian country houses, who in turn was pupil and partner to Raymond Erith. Erith was working on Wivenhoe New Park in Essex when Quinlan Terry joined the office in the early 1960s. Terry worked with Erith and then took over the practice and went on to build highly regarded country houses around England and across the world, many with restrained Palladian style, such as Waverton House and Bibury Court, both in Gloucestershire.[7]

Francis Terry was educated at Stowe School (in the shadow of the architecture of Sir John Vanbrugh, James Gibbs, William Kent, Giovanni Battista Borra, Vincenzo Valdré and Sir John Soane), and studied architecture at Downing College, Cambridge, before spending a period as a professional artist.[8] He qualified as an architect in 1994 and worked for Allan Greenberg Architect in Washington, DC, then spent two decades working for his father Quinlan Terry, becoming a partner in 2004. In 2016 he founded Francis Terry and Associates in order to pursue his own creative path. He had already collaborated with his father on two of the most extraordinary projects of his generation: Kilboy in County Tipperary, Ireland, in 2014, and Ferne Park in Wiltshire, England, for Lord and Lady Rothermere, which finished at the same time.[9]

Eastridge was one of Francis Terry's first independent projects, and combines imaginatively so many strands of the English country-house tradition with modern taste and technology. It has proved to be a happy home for his clients and their family.

↑ A detail of the classical frieze of the chimneypiece in the dining room, picked out in two different stone colours.

3 THE

ARTISTIC EYE

←← The artistic touch: a lively collection on a shelf in the studio of artist Matthew Rice at his characterful Ham Court near Oxford.

→ A Chinese patterned wallpaper in a bedroom at Court of Noke, Shropshire.

COURT OF NOKE

The home of colour and reflections

THERE ARE MANY 'GENTRY' HOUSES of around 1700 that are breathtaking even in their apparent simplicity of form and materials. Court of Noke, in Herefordshire, is one such, a handsomely proportioned red-brick house, in an unspoilt rural landscape near Staunton-on-Arrow. The romantic name of the house is derived from the Old English for 'the place of the oak tree'; it was built on a manorial site mentioned in the Domesday Book.[1] Since 1995 the house has been carefully restored by its current owners, Edward and Emma Bulmer, and the farm buildings provide the studios for Edward's interior decoration and paint-making business.

The house was built originally around 1700 by one George Mason, a 'doctor of physic' from Monmouth who married into a local gentry family and lived on this property from 1673 to 1718. The house was inherited by his daughter, Elizabeth Halhead, who passed it to her son William, who received it in 1749. In the 1770s it passed into the larger estate of the King family of Staunton Park.[2] The house later became a tenant farmhouse and the canal that runs in front of it was linked to a watermill, but otherwise the house was only modestly altered in the nineteenth century, the roof slightly raised to accommodate more servants' rooms and a wing built to the south, creating a U-plan.

The particular beauty of this house is the stretch of canal in front of it – a survival of the original water gardens – which acts as a mirror, a projection of its smiling architectural character.[3] It has been suggested that the canals, restored by the Bulmers, are descendants of an original moated

complex of a medieval manor, but Edward Bulmer feels the pattern of the canals is more suggestive of the sophistication of an early eighteenth-century garden.

The Bulmers bought the house in 1994.[4] Edward is an interior designer and architectural historian, and his wife Emma is an entrepreneur with environmental business interests. Today they collaborate on a popular plastic-free Natural Paint range. Their purchase of the house is a romantic story. Edward Bulmer grew up in an old rectory in Herefordshire, which had been decorated for his parents by David Mlinaric.[5] His family also owned some woodland locally with a simple cabin on it in which they would sometimes stay, and he remembers glimpsing Court of Noke as a child when they were driving to the cabin. When Edward and Emma were married they came to look for a house in this part of England, and by extraordinary coincidence, a mutual friend suggested they look at Court of Noke, which was then about to go on the market.

The house was in need of major repair work, and while the essential character was everywhere evident, it was in a poor state – only one of the original chimney-pieces remained *in situ*. But Edward could bring his own considerable experience to bear on the project. He had trained in the offices of David Mlinaric and Alec Cobbe and worked briefly for the National Trust before taking on projects in his own right, such as the interiors of Home House in London, when it became a club, and Althorp in Northamptonshire, after it was inherited by the present Earl Spencer.[6] He has advised over a number of years at White's in St James's, London, and at Goodwood House in Sussex. He observes that his approach is more like that of an

architect, seeing where important details are missing and sorting out rooms that have lost their original qualities. Emma also brought her formidable project management skills from her business life.

The couple received permission to remove a run-down single-storey addition at the rear of the house and created a handsome family kitchen with a new top-lit eating room and new laundry and boot rooms. Externally, the Bulmers replaced nineteenth-century dormers with a version more appropriate to the age of the house. The roof had been adjusted to provide additional servants' accommodation in the later nineteenth century. They also inserted real windows along the north side. The main elevation of seven bays has three central bays, under a broad pediment, which slightly projects forward. The front has flush-framed sash windows that may be early replacements for cross-windows (there is one such window surviving in the garden hall of the house). Internally, the Bulmers joined two smaller rooms together on the south side of the house to form the elegant Music Room, the principal reception room, which has newly made-up panelling, cornice and chimneypiece, all designed by Edward. He designed much of the furniture too, but there are also fine antique pieces, including a James Wyatt 'Duchesse' seat traced to the 1820s sale at Fonthill Splendens in Wiltshire.

Textiles play an important role in these rooms: in the Music Room the curtains are hand-blocked cotton from Jaipur, and the carpet was woven by David Bamford. The paint colours throughout the house belong to the Bulmers' own Natural Paint range: the green in the Music Room is Pomona and was inspired by the drawing room at Biddesden in Wiltshire. The kitchen's woodwork is French Grey, while the cupboards are Vert de Mer and the walls are Dove.

→ The garden hall is painted in Edward Bulmer's Turquoise, the perfect backdrop for the terracotta bust.

Emma recalls: 'I wanted things to be done and not to have to wait forever, so our children could enjoy growing up here, but there is always something else. A house has a purpose, to be lived in and enjoyed. I also feel the house and garden are very closely linked. The Music Room is very special to me, with its pink leather sofa, Indian bedspreads as curtains and family paintings: Edward's own paintings of India, a portrait of our middle daughter Evie by her elder sister Isabella, and the Georgian portrait of two Arundell boys looking down on us. I think the house has been a creative project for Edward, but it never ends and we are always looking forward to the next thing'.[7]

The elegant dining room was created out of damp, featureless back rooms and overlooks the walled garden: the general effect is more Regency in feel, with a sideboard area framed by plaster cornice brackets, the design of which was modelled on originals by Humphry Repton found at Sheringham Hall in Norfolk. The soft blue paint on the walls is Aquatic and provides an excellent foil to the dark mahogany furniture and the long table with its upholstered chairs. Moulded architraves designed by Edward have also been added to the windows as well as a new dado rail.

The entrance hall (in a more reticent Lilac Pink, almost a stone shade) retains a fine staircase that appears to have been

← A restored sash window with window seat in the Music Room looking out over the canal. The curtains are hand-blocked cotton from Jaipur.

↑ Mellow pinks and greens embellish the Music Room, which also serves as the family drawing room. The colours were inspired in part by the drawing room at Biddesden in Wiltshire. Owner Edward Bulmer designed the panelling and chimneypiece himself.

added in the early eighteenth century, perhaps around 1740. The neo-Greek cornice was added by Edward, who also introduced the classical chimneypiece inlaid with scagliola decoration featuring the flora and fauna that can be found along the nearby River Arrow, executed by Thomas Kennedy (described by John Martin Robinson as 'a modern master of the Georgian craft').[8] Opposite it hangs a towering eighteenth-century hunting scene painted by John Wootton, which effectively brings a vision of nature indoors.

The lobby leading to the garden hall is hung densely with architectural drawings and engravings, in many cases of Herefordshire country houses that have been demolished and lost. The Oak Room, originally the main parlour of the house, retains all its 1730s–40s raised-and-fielded panelling and an elegant chimneypiece with fluted Doric pilasters, and

overmantel. This room has been filled with locally made modern furniture to serve as the family sitting room.

The principal bedrooms are equally carefully judged with ceilings raised and cornices designed by Edward. The Indian Room, which retains an original bolection-moulded chimneypiece, features a fine Pierre Frey tree-of-life textile evocative of old chintz patterns, and has new panelling to dado-rail height. The Chinese Room is hung with a nineteenth-century hand-painted Chinese wallpaper restored by Allyson McDermott (this originally came from Lambton Castle in County Durham, and David Mlinaric helped the Bulmers acquire it).[9] The Bulmers effectively designed the whole room around the paper, including the metal bed frame, in a Chinese style. The landing is adorned with extraordinary black-and-white wildlife photographs taken in Africa by Cherry

Kearton – Edward Bulmer's mother's grandfather – widely recognised as one of the world's first wildlife photographers.[10]

The Bulmers have devoted considerable energy to the garden, creating to the south of the house two enclosed areas, one of which is a rose garden overlooked by the Music Room and family kitchen. Beyond this, there are gardens echoing those seen in early eighteenth-century paintings, and avenues of hornbeam carry the eye outwards to the views beyond. The restoration of the canals has also been a massive task, but one that has clearly given great satisfaction; the next phase includes the repair and renovation of the 1880s farm buildings, including a working watermill.

Court of Noke is a well-loved family home, but it also has a place in the history books for another reason: it is a testing ground for Edward Bulmer Natural Paint, a place where the designer can explore colours against countless details, such as stone flags and wooden floorboards, the very things that are, he says, the 'mainstays of the English country house'.[11] The unspoilt rural setting and the canal gardens provide much of the charm, but the interior especially is an expression of the Bulmers' own taste, and the designs are drawn out from deep explorations of the character and spirit of the house. The rooms are beautifully composed and well used, and depend for much of their effect on their nods to nature both within and without.

↑   The Oak Room, with its panelling dating to the 1730s–40s, is home to a collection of contemporary art and bright, modern furniture.

→→   The dining room space was created by combining nineteenth-century service areas. It is painted a bold green, and the windows are hung with key-patterned curtains.

↑　The modern family kitchen with fittings
and island designed by Edward Bulmer.

↑ The top-lit breakfast room, or informal dining room, was added just off the kitchen and looks out over a rose garden.

← *clockwise from top left:* a carved four-poster bed against a
Pierre Frey tree-of-life textile evocative of old chintz patterns;
the chinoiserie hanging in 'the smallest room'; a detail of a
painted Regency chair; a detail of the principal bathroom.

↑ The entrance hall, looking into the Oak Room,
with walls of Lilac Pink that is almost a stone colour
and hung with a huge eighteenth-century hunting
scene painted by John Wootton.

→ A country house in Norfolk near the coast, Voewood was designed by Edward Schroeder Prior and built in 1903–5 for the Reverend Percy Lloyd. It has strong built-in decorative detail, such as this tile-on-edge patterning.

VOEWOOD

Made by its materials

VOEWOOD BELONGS BOTH TO THE idealism of the early 1900s and to today. It was designed by a talented Arts and Crafts architect, Edward Schroeder Prior.[1] It was built in 1903–5 for the Reverend Percy Lloyd, but like so many country houses, it passed through various institutional uses in the twentieth century, and the magic of its humane and simple interiors seemed destined never to be enjoyed again as the domestic space it was designed to be. However, since 1998 it has been gently restored by rare book dealer Simon Finch as a single-family house, and used for events including the annual Voewood Festival of literature and music. The garden has also been restored following the bones of the original integrated Arts and Crafts plan, with its unusual blend of formal and natural styles.

Finch's interiors have been guided by his own artistic eye, working with specialist builder David Garromane, with whom he removed some internal partitions in order to return the historic interiors to their original volumes.[2] There are a series of judicious and colourful interventions by artist-maker Annabel Grey, who introduced new mosaic floors, pebble-fronted cabinets and murals in bedrooms and bathrooms, which fill the romantic architecture with unexpected theatre.

These imaginative and modern touches are fitting echoes of Prior's original approach. He was an academic and artistic architect who actively sought in his work to put the theories of John Ruskin and William Morris into practice.[3] Prior was a pupil of Richard Norman Shaw, whose office trained many

leading architects of the early twentieth century. He established his own practice in 1880, and was asked to found the school of architecture at Cambridge in 1912. Voewood is perhaps his best-known domestic work and is a hearty and breathtaking sculptural affair.

It is the sheer originality of the composition of the house that is so arresting – some commentators find it too much. Voewood is, in effect, a vivid expression of the admired qualities of sixteenth- and early seventeenth-century manorial architecture combined with an inventive use of local building materials and traditions: field flint left in pebble form, brick, iron-rich carstone and clay tile. As Dan

Cruickshank wrote, Voewood 'embodies a sophisticated and creative use of appropriate history and precedent … It fuses traditional and modern building. It suggests a direction in which British architecture could have gone'.[4] The house and seven-acre garden were also the epitome of the Arts and Crafts spirit, designed as extensions of each other, as if the one grew out of the other. There is a high terrace walk, low dividing walls, ponds and stairs, lime walks and espaliered fruit trees in the enclosed orchard behind the house (the original designs give a flavour of the rigorous geometry connecting the house and the garden and its enclosures).[5]

→ A side view reveals the theatrical, almost baroque, character of the house. The whole was carefully designed within the semi-formal garden so beloved of the Edwardian age.

Percy Lloyd, the original patron, was an Oxford-educated historian cleric, the son of the wealthy publishing entrepreneur Edward Lloyd, who owned newspapers and paper mills, and whose home had been the childhood home of William Morris (Percy Lloyd's brother Edward presented the house to Walthamstow district in north-east London, which converted it to a museum devoted to Morris). Percy Lloyd wanted a new house in Norfolk that combined historical awareness with a contemporary emphasis on artistic values and sunlight.

In the end, Percy Lloyd did not live long in the house he had built; he retired to Italy soon after the death of his wife, Dorothea, and the house was let and then bought by another cleric, the Reverend Frederic Meyrick-Jones, who ran a small private school there. 'Home Place', as it became known, was published in *Country Life* in 1909, which shows that it was furnished as a private residence and that Meyrick-Jones was 'an enthusiastic and discerning collector of furniture … [who had] many specimens of museum quality', which mixed seventeenth-century oak furniture and Middle Eastern textiles.[6]

Prior was an idealist and believed 'that a house should not be a design but a building, conditioned not only by the needs of the man who will live in it, but by the local experience of construction'[7]; and the well-modelled and textured gabled house has a strongly organic flavour and the handling of the materials is noted by all commentators. He was assisted by Randall Wells as clerk of works (who also worked for W.R. Lethaby), and Detmar Blow also played a role. Wells and Blow had collaborated on nearby Happisburgh Hall and shared

Prior's admiration for Ruskin and Morris. The local builder, on whom great responsibility fell under all these discerning eyes, was a Mr Blower.[8]

South-facing and laid out on the butterfly plan of which Prior was a master (following a clever precedent set by Norman Shaw in the design of Chesters, in Northumberland), the residence feels unusually light for an English country house. Indeed, the interiors of Voewood have an almost Mediterranean feeling with their emphasis on the southern aspect and garden and the white plastered walls. The architect made remarkable structural and decorative use of concrete.

The splay of the butterfly plan defines the way the house works internally. Prior had exhibited a model with a butterfly plan at the Royal Academy of Arts, London, in 1895, and soon after built one, known as The Barn, at Exmouth in 1896–97.[9] At Voewood, this happy and expansive plan form is at first concealed on the approach. The main entrance front seems to be a conventional five-bay elevation with a double-height porch, and extending skirt walls hide the magnificent splay of the south front and terraced gardens, which are appreciated only as a visitor passes through to the rooms beyond.

The core of the house, with windows to both the north and south, is a galleried great hall, which was always designed as the capacious principal drawing room, the 'living hall' so popular in Edwardian country-house design. The huge hearth and rounded arched moulded windows again have an almost Mediterranean feel combined with oak columns and beams. The hearth encloses an inglenook fireplace within polished Hopton Wood stone

columns, with fitted seats and decorated with Delft tiles, making it a room within a room for the winter. The house was probably designed more with the summer in mind, however, as the room is open to the cross corridor that gives access to the south-facing terrace (there are also fluted radiators dating to the early 1900s).

A billiard room and a library – now the Music Room – make up the rest of the west range of the plan, with a kitchen, dining room and a pantry, now a cloakroom, on the east. Both the library and the dining room originally connected with loggias that were always known as 'cloisters'. The stout oak staircase with its primitive barley-sugar balusters is surprisingly compact, squeezed into a wedge-shaped part of the plan, but this enhances its rather sculptural quality.

Simon Finch has been a rare book dealer since he was a teenager, and in London has owned bookshops in Mayfair and on Ledbury Road, and an art gallery on Portobello Road. He fell in love with Voewood rather by accident when it was advertised for sale in 1998, when it was still in use as an old people's home, renamed as Thornfield Hall. He had long been thinking of acquiring a house in the country but had not anticipated taking on such an unusual architectural statement. Nonetheless, it became a major labour of love, and he has relished introducing a consistently eclectic feel throughout.

Finch's collection ranges across photographs and prints, with works by Kenny Scharf, Austin Osman Spare, Paula Rego, John Piper, Graham Sutherland and Gerald Brockhurst. A huge oil painting of the *Last Supper* by Brockhurst hangs in the dining room, which is lit by a series of hanging Moroccan lamps, and features

assorted chairs in Arts and Crafts–inspired styles, including some made to designs by Charles Rennie Mackintosh. The 1909 *Country Life* article (thought to be written by Lawrence Weaver but signed only 'W') also noted how the original plan anticipated the opportunity to have a dining room on the terrace. The Music Room – both Simon and his actor son Jack are accomplished guitar players – has a Steinway baby grand piano that once belonged to the impresario Lew Grade. The Music Room is furnished with African textiles and animal skins, while the billiard room, with its deep red walls, is fitted with shelves for books.

Finch wanted above all to preserve the feeling of light and space that he believes was an essential part of the Arts and Crafts vision for the house. Over several years he furnished some seventeen bedrooms with different themes. He was assisted in his revival by Norfolk-based Annabel Grey, a textile designer and artist, who trained at the University of Manchester and the Royal College of Art. Her murals can be seen across England (including on the walls of Marble Arch Underground station in London).[10] Grey brings a remarkable sense of colour and style that responds to the exuberance of the architecture and garden: her vivid mosaic pavement in the eastern loggia is highly original. She also painted the Patchwork Bedroom, which appears to be partly inspired by Gustav Klimt and the tones of the artists of Bloomsbury. Another bedroom, the Green Room, is painted by Chloe Mandy to resemble a densely green glade in a semi-wild garden; it is one of many enjoyable deft touches within Norfolk's own house of fun.

→ *clockwise from top left:* artwork in the great hall; embroidered butterflies on a curtain; the original deep inglenook fireplace in the great hall–like drawing room, decorated with glazed tiles; a Paul Klee–inspired mural decoration by Annabel Grey.

→ This bird's-eye view of The Laskett, Herefordshire, and its gardens, was painted by Jonathan Myles-Lea and celebrates the extensive formal gardens created by Sir Roy Strong and Dr Julia Trevelyan Oman.

THE LASKETT

A garden of memories and stories

EVERY HOUSE HAS ITS OWN STORY, but this one can be told from both inside and out, depending on where you are standing. Some stories have a greater sense of narrative than others. Sir Roy Strong is one of England's most distinctive cultural commentators, and is a former director of both the National Portrait Gallery and Victoria and Albert Museum in London, as well as an author, columnist, High Bailiff of Westminster Abbey, expert on the Elizabethan portrait, and diarist. His column in *Country Life* from 1989 to 1994, musings on garden-making and living in the country, here at The Laskett, offers a vivid portrayal of a particular period of English culture.[1]

The story of Sir Roy's The Laskett began in 1973, just before his appointment to the V&A, when he married the set designer, Julia Trevelyan Oman – famous especially for her work in ballet and opera – and together they bought a plain, early nineteenth-century house not far from Hereford.[2] It was to be a place for work and a place to call home: 'a pink sandstone box from the 1820s which evokes the modesty of a rectory in a novel by Jane Austen', as Sir Roy observes.[3] His late wife jokingly described the original house as 'work rooms with a few state apartments attached'.[4]

The house has evolved considerably in Sir Roy's hands, especially with additional embellishments in 2004–6, so now it feels Palladian at the main front, with pilasters and medallions, while the sides are lightly 'Castle of Otranto' Gothic (a reference to the novel by Horace Walpole, creator of Strawberry Hill House in Twickenham,

←← Every part of the garden tells a story: this is the Silver Jubilee Garden, celebrating the first twenty-five years of the reign of Queen Elizabeth II.

London).[5] The main drawing room and the densely hung cabinet-like anteroom are filled with portraits, either collected by Sir Roy or inherited from his wife's family. Indeed, the drawing room was built partly to accommodate furniture from Julia's family.

The furniture includes a marquetry cabinet and a chair of needlework upholstery, worked by Julia's aunt Carola Oman, the historian and author Lady Lenanton, who had lived at Bride Hall in Hertfordshire (thus the drawing room has been nicknamed 'the state apartment' or 'Bride Hall'). Over the door hangs a portrait of Prince Henry, eldest son of James I, who died young and about whom Sir Roy has written an admired biography. Sir Roy recalls how little money they had to spend on furniture and paintings at first, but 'John Cornforth encouraged me to look carefully and mix things up to create a good decorative effect'.[6]

The drawing room opens into a substantial garden room, with views of the Yew Garden – one of the first parts of the garden established in 1974. There are a number of artworks by John Piper in the house that hint at the English romanticism underlying Sir Roy's outlook, despite his academic roots in the sixteenth century and his love of formality. The breakfast room is hung with engravings of formal gardens, the walls painted yellow and the room furnished with painted Gothic chairs from an earlier house he owned in Brighton.

The original entrance hall doubles as a dining room and is dominated by Paul Brason's bird's-eye view of the house and garden, which gives it a dreamy Italianate aspect – the large sketch for this hangs in the staircase hall, and illustrates the essentially sculptural quality of the four-acre garden.

↑ The main front of the plain Regency house, which has been enlivened with artful Palladian touches designed by Sir Roy himself.

→ Looking along one of the garden's avenues across the fountain court to the side of the house, showing Gothic detail by Sir Roy.

→ The small dining room in the former
entrance hall with another bird's-eye view of
the garden, this one painted by Paul Brason.

One corridor is filled with portraits of
Sir Roy by famous photographers, such
as Sir Cecil Beaton, Norman Parkinson
and Lord Snowdon, another by framed
caricatures and cartoons of him by Sir
Osbert Lancaster, Gerald Scarfe and
Marc Boxer, commemorating the lively
years of his museum directorships ('has
any other museum director appeared in
so many newspaper cartoons I wonder'?
he muses[7]). A large country kitchen lies
at the heart of the house and hints at the
hospitality that has flowed through its
rooms. This is also echoed in the newest
temple in the garden, suitable for shaded
lunch parties at a table facing the long
axis back to the fountain court and house.

The house is filled with books and
pictures, a fitting complement in the
home of two such individuals. As Sir Roy
observes, 'everything in it is charged
with memory'. It is also very comfortable: there is an intimate sitting room in
a Gothic spirit, and a sequence of rooms
upstairs devoted to writing. In 2006,
after the death of Julia, Sir Roy donated
her archive (30,000 designs) to the
Theatre Collection of the University of
Bristol. His own archive is being donated
to the Bodleian Library, of the University
of Oxford.

Sir Roy has spent time refurnishing
these rooms and indeed remodelling
the house. He recorded the experience
in his diaries, and wrote on 23 February
2006: 'I had no intention of doing all this.
It began slowly then accelerated, firstly
because some things had to be done and
then creative energy took over … I was
driven on by the knowledge that nearly
all of those involved were on the edge
of retiring and they were a spectacular
team: the builders Geoff and Gerry Davis,

humorous, inventive, careful with their
work, always able to come up with a solution. It was Geoff who came up with the
Aristocast catalogue filled with historic
plaster moulding by the yard … Geoff
brought in his son Greg, who was able to
run up Georgian Gothick windows'.[8] The
painters were Paul Reeks and his son
Chris: 'Paul has the best colour sense
and taste ever, superb, mixing colours for
every room'.

During this phase Sir Roy inserted a
new staircase hall, painted dark green
and featuring elegant portraits, including
one of himself by Paul Brason; he also
commissioned a huge tableau painting by
Richard Shirley Smith to celebrate Julia's
career and the garden. French windows
in the drawing room have brought in more
light, and he has introduced a new chimneypiece, added plasterwork to the ceiling
and hung yellow curtains (made up by
Sue Leyshon-James), creating a Soanian
effect. The hall was converted into the
dining room, with additional columns
and tiled floors. Overall, Sir Roy admits
to being influenced by John Fowler's
'country-house look', a style 'which could
make inexpensive things look beautiful'
and helped at The Laskett by rooms peppered with portraits and with flowers.[9]

Even if the garden has an Italianate
flavour, it cannot be denied that, in the
English way, the house is intimately connected with the garden. The latter is a
remarkable creation, and, perhaps even
more than the house, is a narrative work,
speaking of the avenues of Sir Roy's and
Julia's careers and interests. It is a work
of art, and England is one of its binding
themes.

That the garden was a child of the
1970s is often a surprise to visitors, but

↑ The densely hung anteroom has some of the finest portraits in Sir Roy's collection.

↑ The heavy curtain drapes of the landing offer an enjoyable moment of theatre on the first floor of the Laskett.

↑ One of the 'working rooms' of the house where
Sir Roy's books on art and history are researched.

← ← The finely composed Nymphaeum garden
with a glimpse of the wider landscape beyond.

in many ways that is the point of it: 'it was a period of deep gloom, and I clearly remember that the act of planting a garden was a deliberate and defiant one'.[10] The couple bought the house in 'the period of the fall of the Heath government, the oil crisis, and industrial and social unrest', a time of great uncertainty that was reflected in the first exhibition Sir Roy and his team put on at the V&A, *The Destruction of the Country House*, in 1974, which shocked the nation into a sense of what had been lost.

Sir Roy had a deep personal conviction that the most English of 'art forms, the classic English country house garden, would go on'.[11] His garden has been inspired by late Stuart gardens recorded by Johannes Kip in *Nouveau Théâtre de Grande Bretagne* (1715), and the photographs in Charles Latham's *In English Homes* (1904), as well as the gardens of friends Sir Cecil Beaton and John Fowler. In fact, he recalls that Beaton was 'the first person ever to walk me round a garden' at his house in Reddish, Greater Manchester.[12] The Villa Lante at Bagnaia, near Viterbo, central Italy, and the garden at Hidcote in Gloucestershire have also had an affect on this extraordinary place. Most influential was Fowler's creation at King John's Hunting Lodge in Hampshire, which was 'the most perfectly articulated small garden I have ever seen'.[13]

For the next decade and a half, much of the work lay in the creation of hedges, screens and the overall shape. This included the installation of temples, follies and sculpture that entertain both the eye and the mind – a mixture of surprise and grand effect:[14] from the *Die Fledermaus* walk celebrating Julia Trevelyan Oman's 1983 designs

for Johann Strauss's operetta at the Royal Opera House, London, to the Silver Jubilee Garden that honoured the Queen in 1977; the Elizabeth Tudor Walk, named after Elizabeth I; the Ashton Arbour, commemorating their friend Sir Frederick Ashton and Julia Trevelyan Oman's designs for *A Month in the Country* (1976), and the ballet based on Sir Edward Elgar's *Variations*; and a 'V&A' Temple recalling Sir Roy's directorship of the Victoria and Albert Museum from 1974 to 1987 (with a plaque carved by Simon Verity). Among the many sculptures is a monument to William Shakespeare (Sir Roy was awarded the Shakespeare Prize in 1980) and another to Henry II, a figure from Westminster Abbey, where Sir Roy held the position of High Bailiff.

The Laskett and its gardens are the result of four decades of design and evolution; they are very English, romantic and wittily autobiographical. But, especially in the garden, autobiography is only part of the narrative, for the references are stepping-off points to new creations that have made their own memorable visual stories. Sir Roy has resolved to leave the house this year, and the garden will be preserved by a charitable trust, Perrennial, as a cultural landmark in the story of the English garden.

→ *clockwise from top left:* the new staircase hall; a group of icons; prints and engravings of formal gardens hanging in the yellow breakfast room; an embroidered chair from Bride Hall in Hertfordshire.

ON GARDENS

The English country house is defined in many people's minds by its relationship to the garden: indeed, a love of gardening has come to be seen almost as part of the English character.[1] The garden provides a connection with nature but also represents nature tamed for enjoyment and leisure. The houses in this book have gardens of widely differing characters – formal, informal, picturesque, moated, neo-Japanese; here delicacy, there more densely framed by sculpted yew topiary – but they are united by their connection to the amenity of a country house.

What seems inescapable in them all is the sense of a meeting between the formal and informal, and how the English country house, large or small, is entirely interconnected with its garden. The garden spaces provide more 'rooms' for socialising, privacy, intimacy and delight; unlike the interiors of the house, they change with the seasons, grow and need constant attention. They also frame the views of the landscape and often merge imperceptibly into the surrounding meadows and woodlands. Flowers invade the houses in arrangements that bring colour and perfume inside, often setting up unexpected dialogues with fabrics, chintzes and wallpapers, so ubiquitous are the images of nature inside.

England's generally temperate climate plays a key role in this particular quality. There is also a meeting of many strands, for the English garden, like the English interior, is influenced by so many ideas and styles from other parts of the world: Italy and ideals of classicism, French painters, French and Italian formal gardens, the Middle East, India (Sezincote), Japan (Heale House) and China, as well as plants from Alpine regions, pines from the Americas, and modern planting ideas from Holland and Germany. The English country-house garden has always been a melting pot of ideas and experiences, and often carries a degree of biographical narrative of its own, about the people who have shaped it, whether a new or an old garden (nowhere encountered more enjoyably than at The Laskett).

→ The mellow-textured terraced garden of
Haddon Hall in Derbyshire combines modern
and ancient approaches and a beguiling softness
of character.

The history of the English country-house garden is a long one, and it is clear that early medieval gardens were often both productive, containing medicinal herbs and fruit, and ornamental, and always had a social dynamic as places for entertainment and retreat.[2] Manuscript illuminations include depictions of the *hortus conclusus*, an enclosed or protected garden directly linked to castle or house, possibly influenced by the Islamic world 'paradise garden', which was designed to be a reflection of heaven on earth.[3] These gardens were also distinct from fenced hunting parks set aside for sport.

On a more extensive scale and sited so they could be seen and enjoyed from the state rooms, Tudor palace and great house gardens were an elaboration of these earlier enclosed gardens, featuring patterned knot gardens, trellised arbours and tunnels.[4] From the late sixteenth century, imports of Italian features, grottoes and water effects began to enhance the English repertoire. During the seventeenth century the 'pleasure garden', attached to a country house, became an ever more vital canvas for keeping up with fashionable taste. In Renaissance thinking the garden was seen as 'a living encyclopaedia of God's creation', as well as an indicator of social status and place of entertainment.[5]

After the Restoration of the Stuart monarchy in 1660, there was a more monumental approach to gardening and landscaping, with axial rides and avenues influenced by French taste (and the work of André Le Nôtre). These ambitious gardens are recorded in Leonard Knyff and Jan Kip's *Britannia Illustrata* (1707), where the house is often, as one early twentieth-century author Hermann Muthesius observed, 'a tiny element appearing to float in a much larger ocean of ornamental and pleasure gardens'.[6] There were certain notable English characteristics such as grass parterres made with turf, gravel and sand (known as 'parterre à l'Angloise' across Europe). The English always seem to have been drawn to a more naturalistic view of gardening, as championed by John Evelyn, especially in his *Sylva* of 1664.[7]

In the early eighteenth century the naturalistic approach was ever more celebrated even in an age still dominated by long avenues and vistas. The politician and philosopher Anthony Ashley Cooper, the 3rd Earl of Shaftesbury, wrote in *The Moralists* (1709), celebrating 'things of a natural kind: where neither art nor the Conceit and Caprice of man has spoil'd their genuine order'.[8] The essayist Joseph Addison also rejected the 'artificial' and openly embraced a new vision in *The Spectator* in 1712: 'why not may a Whole Estate be thrown into a kind of garden by frequent plantations? [...] If the *natural* embroidery of the meadows were helped and improved by some small additions of Art … a man might make a pretty Landscape of his own possessions'.[9] This merging of garden and estate landscape is a key leitmotif of the English country-house garden, as a place both of views and nature, as well as of trees, flowers and enclosure.

Agricultural improvement and the laying out of parks and gardens in the Georgian age was closely associated with the fashion for building new houses. The cultural map provided by classical literature and the Grand Tour meant that classical symbolism provided a strong thread for the gardens, which were enlivened with temples, grottoes and statuary. Stephen Switzer wrote in 1718, 'all the adjacent country [should] be laid open to view',[10] and the connection with wider tree planting was key. He saw it as something almost patriotic, thus: 'gardening can speak proper English'.[11]

Horace Walpole in 'On the History of Modern Taste in Gardening' (1780) thought that William Kent was 'painter enough to taste the charms of landscapes' and admired how he had 'leaped the fence, and saw that all nature was a garden'.[12] But nature always seems to need enhancement, and during the 1730s a taste for the exotic introduced 'Chinese', 'Turkish', rustic and Gothic structures alongside the classical. The country-house garden became a circuit of dream-like escapes and episodes of different moods and sensations, as seen at Painshill or at Stourhead, in the latter case also influenced by the painting of Claude Lorrain and Nicolas Poussin.[13]

From the increasingly painterly vision of the garden grew the pastoral landscape style of Lancelot 'Capability' Brown. Brown worked for Lord Cobham at Stowe, initially on Kent's designs, but he 'envisaged his landscapes in broad, bold sweeps and on a scale far beyond that of Kent'.[14] Walpole acutely noted how in visiting Brown's gardens, 'every journey is made through a succession of pictures', something echoed in many of the gardens in this book, even if not on the vast scale of some eighteenth-century gardens.[15]

Humphry Repton, a leading landscape designer from 1788, continued with Brown's pastoral sweeps, but added a degree of return to formality around the house and flower gardens as part of the amenity of a country house. Repton prepared his famous 'Red Books', with their 'before' and 'after' views, but, more significantly perhaps, also committed his ideas to print in several books, unlike Brown.[16] Despite being embroiled in the famous 'picturesque controversy', which was rooted in ideas about the beauty of nature over contrivance, Repton had a lasting influence.

J.C. Loudon played an important role in the 'gardenesque' approach, whereby planting was done in a manner that was not mistaken for natural growth, but in which the exotics and specimens stood out: Alpine plants, Chinese rhododendrons, American pines. From the 1830s, there was a new fashion for Italianate gardening, drawing on Jacobean and Caroline models as well as the French parterre tradition.

Late Victorians developed a distinct admiration for the romantic gardens, terraces and overgrown yews associated with the older English manor house. This same romanticism fed directly into the values of the Arts and Crafts Movement, and most notably in the memorable collaboration between Gertrude Jekyll and Edwin Lutyens, in which architecture and gardens were tightly integrated in a semi-formal manner softened by plantings. This Arts and Crafts model was also in part a celebration of the cottage garden,[17] which suited a certain ideal of Englishness and has had a long and enduring influence.

Gardens defined the English country house for some commentators. Hermann Muthesius wrote in *The English House* (1904–5): 'The English house lies in the midst of flower gardens … looking on to broad green lawns which radiate the energy and peace of nature'.[18] Both Vann and Voewood are living expressions of these early twentieth-century approaches to gardening, which, although they evolved with later generations and owners, have remained inescapably romantic places. Beckley Park, too, with its moated gardens and sculpted yew topiary, is a direct link to that very English sensibility of the Edwardian era.

The post-war country-house garden required gardening in a different world; the large staffs, known for centuries, even in minor country houses, quickly dropped away to no more than a handful or even just one person. But this had a most unexpected effect, as Tim Richardson has written: 'it has to be said that many garden owners grasped the opportunity with both hands, and a strong culture of gentry gardening emerged'.[19] Vita Sackville-West perhaps best exemplifies this 'gentry gardening'. At Sissinghurst she created one of the most famous gardens, which she worked with her husband, Sir Harold Nicolson: he provided the architectural layout, and she the plants. Together they aimed at achieving 'the strictest formality of design [combined] with the maximum informality of planting'.[20]

English gardening in the later twentieth century was shaped by an interest in flowers, as championed by Rosemary Verey (and gardeners like Rupert Golby at Eastridge), and a revival of formality, notably in the writings of Sir Roy Strong and at The Laskett, the garden he created in Herefordshire. In the post-war years both Heale House and Sezincote have gardens that have evolved in remarkable ways within their historic frameworks: Lady Anne Rasch and her daughter-in-law Frances, at Heale, and at Sezincote, Lady Kleinwort and her daughter Suki Peake, with advice from Graham Thomas. The gardens of Chyknell were laid out by Russell Page in the early 1950s, framing both house and landscape views – Page spoke of designing a garden 'as an artist composing a picture'.[21]

More recently, ideas from German and Dutch garden design have also led to a new emphasis on form and structure, while the romantic streak remains strong in many English country-house gardens, especially those touched by designers such as Julian and Isabel Bannerman. In this book, Simon Johnson's formal gardens at Pitshill are the perfect complement to the restored Georgian house, while the abundant planting of the garden at Lake House, on which Arabella Lennox-Boyd advised, frames the approaches to the building beautifully. The new ornamental vegetable garden at fourteenth-century Ham Court brings us almost back to the medieval origins of the English country-house garden.

The gardens in this book are places of reflection and fun, repose and retreat from urban life, of regeneration and relaxation. They are also places that engage the spirit and imagination, such as the stylish plantings at Walcot and Heale and the work by Arne Maynard at Haddon Hall. They are places too for flights of fancy, as with the new 'Gothick' tower at Wolverton. John Evelyn, one of the earliest of the great gentry gardeners, wrote in 1669: 'Gardening is a labour full of tranquillity and satisfaction; natural and instructive, and as such contributes to the most serious contemplation, experience, health and longevity'.[22] The English country-house garden is not an object in the landscape or an appendage to the house; it is as one with the house, part of a way of life.

DRAYCOT HOUSE

A country retreat

DRAYCOT HOUSE LIES IN A REMOTE hamlet in Wiltshire, immediately below the scarp of the Marlborough Downs. This region, situated between London and Bath, is a very green part of England, an area once particularly loved by the landscape painter Paul Nash. The hamlet of Draycot Foliat bears a name that dates from the early fourteenth century and commemorates an otherwise forgotten landholding family of the time.[1] The hamlet almost faded away during the expansion of sheep farming in the sixteenth century, when Draycot Foliat's medieval church was demolished, and the parish became joined to neighbouring Chiseldon. Today, Draycot Foliat is formed around two principal houses, the stone house of Sheppard's Farm, dating from the seventeenth century, and the elegant Draycot House, which is thought to have replaced an earlier manor house that stood here, close to the site of the old church.

Draycot House is a mellow, red-brick seven-bay house, with a slate roof punctuated by dormers. It most probably dates from the first quarter of the eighteenth century and its imposing central doorway is flanked by columns and surmounted by a scrolled pediment, framing a stone urn dappled with lichen. Evidence of timber framing within the house makes it clear that this was a refacing of a sixteenth-century house.[2] The grandeur of the doorcase is surprising and perhaps suggests a remodelling for an eldest son, or the creation of a dower house – it is rather too smart for a farmhouse and more like that of a rectory in character.

← The main stone doorcase of Draycot House is of some elegance and suggests the house was originally designed for a person of status.

↓ The seven-bay front of the circa 1700 red-brick house, which encased an earlier, probably sixteenth-century house that stood here originally.

Draycot House is part of the Burderop Park estate, owned by the Calley family from the seventeenth century onwards. The estate was inherited in the 1970s by Robert Langton, who lived in Draycot House, with his wife Julia, before they moved to Burderop Park itself. Since 2006 Draycot House has been the home of leading interior designer Emily Todhunter, with her husband, Manoli Olympitis, and their three children. It forms a happy family retreat from business, and a base for riding. They keep three horses in the stables, and the house teems with dogs, cats, chickens and doves. As Todhunter says: 'We have a house in London, but this is undoubtedly the place we all think of as home.'[3]

Emily Todhunter has carved an enviable reputation in the interior-design field, with clients in London, across the UK and around the world. She worked on Raymond Blanc's renowned Belmond Le Manoir aux Quat'Saisons and, more recently, on the high Victorian moated Madresfield Court in Worcestershire, which she describes as: 'a completely magical house, beloved of Evelyn Waugh' which had been inherited by her clients.[4] Her firm recovered and revamped furniture retrieved from the attics in good-quality material, used strong colours, especially in the bedrooms, and 'just helped make the old house comfortable'. She has also worked alongside leading architects, including Quinlan Terry and George Saumarez Smith.

Country houses have been an important feature in Todhunter's life since she grew up in The Old Rectory, Farnborough in Berkshire, a delectable 1749 house. Her parents created a famous garden around this delightful red-brick house, previously the beloved home of John Betjeman,[5] who lived there with his family from 1945 to 1951. Draycot House, with its mellow brick and segmental-headed sash windows, echoes some of its character.

'The Old Rectory has been a huge influence on me', says Todhunter, 'I had the happiest of childhoods there. My mother, Caroline, is a painter who used to paint backdrops for Tony Snowdon, and also an artist, illustrating gardening columns in the *Tatler*. We were surrounded by good furniture and paintings. It was a very different upbringing to my husband's, who is Greek, but he loves Draycot, as do our children'.[6]

Todhunter's career developed somewhat unexpectedly after she trained in painting effects alongside Chelsea-based decorator Jim Smart, a colourist who worked for John Fowler. Jim was 'a great cockney character' who taught her the skills of mixing paints, ragging, rolling and sponging, and she later set up her own specialist decorative firm, which did gilding and painted apricot-coloured drawing rooms and murals of Tuscan scenes. She recalls 'the English look then being much in vogue in New

←← A corner of Draycot House's intimate country drawing room with comfortable sofas and walls hung with landscape paintings.

↑ The panelled entrance hall with a round table loaded with inviting piles of fine books. A view of a Greek island hangs over the fireplace.

York. I worked there a lot, and often became a kind of unofficial rep for the interior designers'.[7] In the end, she spent so much time on the home sites that she became interested in decorating the interiors herself.

She was commissioned in 1988 to design the interior of the Au Bar nightclub in New York – 'I probably got the job by spending too much time in nightclubs' – and famously cribbed the style of a London gentlemen's club.[8] After that, she was offered work on a series of large apartments on Park Avenue and Fifth Avenue, to which she brought a touch of English style to her clients' furniture and painting collections. Returning to London in 1990, Todhunter again landed a series of prestigious commissions both for

private houses and popular restaurants, including Daphne's and Christopher's in London.

She was commissioned by the writer Nigel Nicolson to work on his private apartments at Sissinghurst, the Kent house created in the 1930s from the ruins of a larger sixteenth-century complex by Nigel's parents, Harold Nicolson and Vita Sackville-West.[9] 'Nigel gave me a brief to make Sissinghurst look rural but not rustic', she recalls. 'He wrote me a letter to say he thought the colour we had created, "Emily Green", would be at Sissinghurst for generations to come'.[10] In 1998 Todhunter entered into a partnership with the designer Kate Earle.

At Draycot House every room and piece of furniture hints at the combination

of style and comfort that underlines Todhunter's work, and everything is engagingly understated. 'The house has to work for a family, and we could not have anything too precious on show. You want it to work as well on a cold winter's night as on a lovely summer's day', she says. 'The important thing in a country house is always atmosphere and the effect that it has on you when you walk in. Country-house style today still draws on tradition and personality, but contemporary taste means that there is slightly less pattern, less carpet, cleaner lines, but good colours remain of central importance. In the end, the cosiness and comfort appropriate to the life you live is also significant'.[11]

The entrance hall's late seventeenth-century-style raised-and-fielded panelling was added by the Langtons, and makes a good background to mid-twentieth-century oil paintings and drawings that include views of the Greek islands. A round dining table with Regency-style chairs is piled with large tomes of art and design. In this room also hangs a 1998 portrait of Todhunter's father, Michael, by John Merton.[12] The staircase is densely hung with engravings of hunting scenes, as well as a view of the Greek island of Ithaca, where her father built a house that was the setting for many happy childhood holidays.

The drawing room has pale biscuit-coloured walls, a leather-covered club fender and an ottoman upholstered in a Todhunter-designed printed suede, which is similarly crowded with many art and design books. One of the comfortably upholstered sofas and chairs is chintz-covered, and there is an early eighteenth-century shell-headed niche, with curved shelves displaying early Tiffany glass bulbs. The decorative gaming table came from her husband's family home in Constantinople. There are no curtains in these south-facing rooms, as the family uses the timber shutters. Pictures include a painting by Rose Hilton, a drawing by Duncan Grant and prints by David Roberts: 'not heirlooms, really hand-me-downs!' The drawing room has fabric-covered walls in a sort of 'non colour' pale yellowy green 'that is more pear than apple'.[13]

The family kitchen is practical – 'our children insist this room never changes; it's the heart of our life here' – and features an Aga and a built-in light-oak dresser filled with china and walls hung with still-life paintings of jugs and pots. Three south-facing first-floor rooms have simple raised-and-fielded panelling that probably dates to the early 1800s, painted in pale colours.

The garden to the south of the house is principally laid to lawn, framed by deep and profuse borders. The horses are kept in a brick stable block at the back of the house, built in the 1970s for the Langtons in a classical style. There is a series of barns related to the house, one of which is occupied by sculptor Charlie Langton as a studio, where he works on equestrian and animal sculptures.

This is a simple, fine house, characterful in its setting and details and full of artistic touches and stylish comfort, where contemporary furniture and paintings are mixed with old family pieces. There is a strong sense of it being the place for family retreat and recuperation, alongside visits from friends and the wider family. Draycot House also exemplifies Emily Todhunter's approach to her work, which is that a house should function well, be comfortable and, above all, be enjoyed.

→ *clockwise from top left:* a view into the principal bathroom; the main bedroom, with its portrait of a lurcher; a view from the family sitting room through to the hall; a detail showing the circa 1700 wainscot.

→ Playful, neo-medievalist tiles designed by artist, illustrator and entrepreneur Matthew Rice for the family kitchen of his home, Ham Court, near Oxford.

HAM COURT

Castle of fragments

HAM COURT IS A FRAGMENT OF THE early fourteenth-century Bampton Castle built for Aymer de Valence, 2nd Earl of Pembroke, who received a licence to crenellate in 1315.[1] The current house was formed in the later seventeenth century from the surviving western gatehouse, a section of former lodgings and part of an original curtain wall. The house was much reduced in the eighteenth century and then a new gabled south front added, after it was acquired as a tenant farm by Jesus College, Oxford. Ham Court has recently been revived in a sensitive restoration and has gained something of the air of a French manor house. It is the home of painter, designer, writer and entrepreneur Matthew Rice, who has given it the attention an artist might apply but combined with the practicality of a businessman.

The sculpted presence of the house shines out across the water of a restored moat, and the fields surrounding it bristle with the promise of 11,000 trees that have been planted since 2011.[2] Rice observes that the new trees have already helped entice wildlife back to the property, especially songbirds. He inherited his artistic skills from his parents, designer Pat Albeck and set and costume designer, Peter Rice.

Although Matthew Rice grew up in London, he was much influenced by life at the family's weekend cottage on the Stansted Park estate in Sussex, where he developed a love of shooting and all aspects of a country existence, and a happily rural education at Bedales in Hampshire. A regular contributor to *Country Life*, he is author of a number

← ← Ham Court is formed from an early fourteenth-century gatehouse and lodgings that were part of Bampton Castle; the surviving fragment was extended in the nineteenth century to form a substantial farmhouse, here seen from its productive vegetable garden.

of acclaimed books on architecture and architectural history, which he illustrates himself, including *Village Buildings of Britain* (2001), *Rice's Architectural Primer* (2009) and *Oxford* (2020).[3]

Rice revels in the eccentric character of Ham Court and its redolent sense of history, even though he admits that one of the aspects that appeals to him is that it is not an overlarge house. It is nonetheless a tangible link with the life of one of England's great medieval noblemen, Aymer de Valence, a most remarkable military commander of the late thirteenth century.

De Valence also extended his father's famous border castle of Goodrich, in Herefordshire, with new defensive walls, while upgrading the core into a nobleman's residence (although still defensible).[4] Some experts think that the castle at Bampton may well have been larger than Goodrich.[5] A cousin to Edward I of England, De Valence was a commander in the army that defeated Robert I of Scotland, and his extensive landed estates spread over England, Wales and France. On the death of his mother in 1307 he became the 2nd Earl of Pembroke. In the seventeenth century Anthony A. Wood described Bampton Castle as 'a quadrangular building moated with a tower at each corner and a gate house of tower-like character to the west and east side'. This was partly in ruins by 1664, and a large portion of the castle was demolished in 1789.[6]

Rice began the Ham Court project with his former wife, the potter Emma Bridgewater, with whom he founded and ran the eponymous pottery business that has so enhanced English kitchens and country life. The couple were looking for somewhere they could have a home and a working studio space which was in reasonable distance of their factory at Stoke-on-Trent (their previous home had been an old rectory in Norfolk, and they also lived for a time in Oxford). Rice recalls: 'we bought Ham Court in 2011, moved here in 2013, camped for a while in the entirely unmodernised house and then moved back out into the neighbouring barn, which we had converted as a house and studio we could occupy during works to the main house'.[7]

The couple separated in 2017, but Matthew Rice has carried on the restoration and revival of this beguiling and eccentric house, which remains an enjoyable retreat and place of renewal for him and the extended visits he receives from his four adult children and friends. Not surprisingly, his artistic eye has been the guiding force for the work to the house, much of which has been achieved with the help of an experienced local builder, Andy Cartlidge of Oaktree Renovations.

The approach drive from the west is framed by plain gate piers and leads straight to the house through a broad farm court with a long barn on the left-hand side (converted to residential and studio use). The Earl of Pembroke's one-time castle gatehouse forms the focus of the house in front of the visitor, and its story is easily traceable in the stonework, the composition enhanced by the crenellated stone stair tower and a steeply sloping stone-slate roof that confirms an impression of weathered antiquity (a late seventeenth-century drawing shows the survival of more crenellation at that date).[8]

The bucolic atmosphere of the well-weathered building is heightened by its

→ Set in silver waters: Matthew Rice has also restored the broad moat that still borders the house on two sides.

imaginative gardens, just to the north-west of the house, which have been established in a relatively short time, composed with an artist's eye. From the very beginning of the project, Rice was determined to lay the foundations for a large, productive vegetable garden, but in fact he has created two kitchen gardens planted with a mix of herbs and vegetables of all kinds, including decorative plants such as lavender, sweet peas and varieties of marigold: 'Art Shades' and 'Indian Prince'.[9]

These gardens, which fall between the house and the barns, are both practical and intended to be enjoyed by family or guests taking an evening stroll through colour and scent. The wider setting of the

house is more rustic still, with paddocks and trees and a broad stretch of water providing fine reflections of the house and its huge ancient horse chestnut. Rice observes: 'This restoration of the historic moat setting has been a very important part of the project for me'.[10]

There is also what Rice calls a small 'toy' farm, and he keeps some Hereford cattle, Jacob sheep and Berkshire pigs, both for the larder and to enrich the environment, encouraging insects and invertebrates, but also for that incidental animation around a house of which the garden designer Humphry Repton was so acutely aware. Rice says: 'they are so useful, to fertilise the garden and eat the waste'.[11] This has all helped re-establish

↑ The kitchen required careful intervention to restore its original proportions, with its handsome stone-flagged floor, simple oak table and Gustavian bench.

→ *clockwise from top left:* stone vaulting in the master bedroom; the doorway linking the nineteenth century with the medieval; the stone spiral staircase; the one surviving arrow slit.

↑　The joy of simple things: shelves and shelves
of country crockery, decoy ducks and (at the
top) china of Matthew Rice's own design.

↑ The grand piano in the bay window of the drawing room, part of the nineteenth-century additions to Ham Court.

the rustic character of his home, which had become the linchpin of a typically intensive modern farming operation in the late twentieth century. A series of fine barns and stables is situated to the north and west of the house, some of which date back to the seventeenth century.

Inside, the house has a fresh, unpretentious atmosphere: part dream cottage, part French hunting lodge. The entrance hall is a simple whitewashed space, while the early fourteenth-century gateway was divided horizontally to form a dining room on the ground floor and the two-bay vaulted master bedroom above. The sheer quality of the stonework of the moulded piers visible on the inside face of the outside wall of the dining room is indicative of the quality of the original project for the Earl of Pembroke's new great house.

Rice has kept the dining room very plain, with whitewashed walls and traditional furniture suggestive of an Arts and Crafts house of the early twentieth century; furnishings fit simply into the room, such as a sideboard from Eastern Europe painted a pale grey. It is loaded with Tuscan-style slipware made in the Stoke-on-Trent Emma Bridgwater factory, and an eighteenth-century buffet is filled with coloured glass. The south-facing 1860s gabled, stone addition, in a loosely neo-Tudor manner, undoubtedly provided a series of well-proportioned and useful rooms.

The associated kitchen, on the east side of the house, was a much-divided space and belonged to a very different era, when servants ran even the household of a prosperous tenant farmer. Rice removed these partitions and a modern concrete floor to reveal the original flagstones underneath. He designed the scrubbed-oak kitchen table himself, choosing the wood from the sawmill at Eynsham. The tiles behind the Aga and the sink have been designed especially by Rice to depict Ham Court as a castle before its reduction, Aymer de Valence on horseback and a roundel taken from his tomb in Westminster Abbey.

One first-floor room retains a high-quality chimneypiece of the early fourteenth century, and on the ground floor is a huge-scaled, arrow-slit window, revealed by the removal of a cupboard, that brings light into an otherwise plain pink-washed corridor. The principal south-facing 1860s rooms include a large well-lit drawing room, with a grand piano bought by Rice's grandfather directly from Bechstein in the 1930s, and a study, perhaps once a dining room but now a well-filled library-studio where Rice works on his architectural books and distinctive watercolour studies of buildings. The house is filled with paintings by himself, and by other members of his family and friends: in his own master bedroom are monochrome paintings of north Italian architecture by his father Peter Rice, from the 1950s.

Ham Court is the house of an artist. It was crafted first by medieval masons for a grandee, adapted in the seventeenth century, then much reduced in the eighteenth century, before being given a set of useful rooms in the mid-nineteenth century. Matthew Rice's revival of the building has been ingenious and imaginative: vistas through the house are composed with an artistic eye, and every interior has the considered feel of a still-life painting, while also giving signs of being much enjoyed by the owner, family and friends.

↑ Four views of the master bedroom and adjoining bathroom that form the upper volume of the early fourteenth-century castle gateway.

NORTH FARM

Pattern of comfort

NORTH FARM IS A PLEASANT, smiling, rambling nineteenth-century farmhouse in County Durham, with its own cluster of working and historic barns and stables. Part of one of the stone barns was originally a thirteenth-century chapel, serving a medieval village that has long since vanished beneath the lumpy contours of the surrounding fields.[1] North Farm was historically a working tenant farm on the Walworth Castle estate. The biographer Philip Eade inherited half of what was left of the estate in 1979 from a cousin, Peter Eade, a theatrical agent who had grown up at Low Walworth Hall.[2] The other half remained in the ownership of Philip's father, Charles Aylmer Eade (always known as 'Tommy').

The author of a series of well-received biographies of twentieth-century figures from the young Prince Philip to Evelyn Waugh,[3] Philip Eade was at first resistant to investing much in a house whose potential had previously escaped him. However, he admits to having eventually enjoyed the project of rehabilitating this old family property. It was Eade's wife, Rita Konig, interior designer daughter of decorating doyenne Nina Campbell, who suggested it would be an interesting challenge to make their own country retreat out of the characterful, long, low stone farmhouse that had such strong associations with the Eade family, who had owned the Walworth estate since 1775. Their Aylmer ancestors at Walworth were a rich mix who clearly appeal to Eade's biographer's instincts: Newcastle industrialists, Durham clerics and Irish landed gentry.

→ This set of shelving in the family kitchen was designed originally for a French bakery; the adjoining scullery features vertical boarding.

The castle itself was mostly built in the seventeenth century and remodelled in the 1860s.[4] It was sold off in 1950 (along with two-thirds of the land), became a boarding school and is now a hotel. Eade's father and grandfather were both agents to Lord Barnard's estates in Shropshire, so they never lived at Walworth, and Philip Eade himself grew up in that other county.

The recent restoration project was a bigger task than the Eades had foreseen, as although it was stoutly built in stone and quietly handsome in the way of such houses, it had never been fully modernised and required extra rooms to make it work for today's family life and entertaining. They planned the house to be as comfortable and welcoming as possible, suitable for their own needs and at the same time able to expand easily to fill up at weekends with friends and wider family – it now has efficient plumbing, seven bedrooms and sleeps fourteen.

↑ The rambling stone farmhouse, part of an estate owned by Mr Eade's family since the eighteenth century, has been remodelled to provide a new large family kitchen on the side, and extra bedrooms and bathrooms above.

←← The drawing room was formed from the original entrance hall of the house. The walls are painted Invisible Green, an Edward Bulmer colour; the sofa and chairs are arranged for relaxing weekends and hospitable conversation.

↑ The long oak table of the new kitchen is designed for dinner parties as well as everyday living. The lithograph of an artichoke is by Sarah Graham.

↑ The long dresser is designed by Christopher
Howe for Plain English and painted dark.

With a judicious extension added over what were single-storey cart sheds and stores on the north side of the house, the Eades have created a large, light-filled family kitchen that can also serve as a dining room, as well as two bedrooms and a bathroom upstairs. They remodelled a very modest staircase to something more in the manner of a late seventeenth-century stair, with cut balusters approached from a new entrance hall, which improved the flow of the house (this latter room opening into a boot room). The overall project took about two years and was completed just before Christmas 2018. Konig has enjoyed reviving this old house, and is now turning her attention to the wider garden setting.

The glowing and inviting interiors of the house have had the benefit of an expert eye. Konig has carved out an enviable reputation for interior design with a distinctive style full of colour and comfort.[5] Thus the interiors of North Farm have been informed by a very personal ideal of understated country-house style but with a brightness and a dose of bold colour and pattern that give it a modern chicness. This echoes the underlying approach taken in many country houses today by new generations. Nature is clearly a central inspiration, both in the earth tones of the principal rooms and the floral and organic themes in curtains and fabrics in the bedrooms.

There is also a theme of relaxed hospitality here, and there are a generous number of bedrooms on the first floor, with a strong emphasis on 'good linen and good headboards'.[6] Through these rooms too are woven memories of the other family houses, in the form of artworks on the walls, including watercolour views of old Walworth Castle and paintings by Graham Rust of Tyringham Park in Buckinghamshire, the home of Konig's grandparents, along with portraits and Eade family photographs that occupy discreet corners.

Konig naturally draws on her own decades of experience at the front line of interior decoration, and acknowledges both the influence of her mother, as well as houses they visited when she was a child. She was brought up principally in London but recalls especially how they 'spent a lot of holidays in Scotland when I was growing up, and I have particular memories of the bedrooms at Beaufort Castle, near Inverness, home of the Lovats, who were very good friends of my mother's; and Virginia Fraser's style was understated but so memorable, comfortable but full of contrasts, and I especially remember the unexpected way in which they mixed furniture of different scales and periods – and textiles of different patterns'.[7]

North Farm is south-facing, and in the summer the principal rooms are naturally full of light: their furniture is deliberately mixed in scale and date, and patterns throw up interesting contrasts – curtains are heavy, fitting for a remote rural house (including Jean Monro fabrics, such as 'Hydrangea' and 'Rose' chintzes' and 'Bowness' linen). The new entrance hall on the north side of the house has a fresh, modern feel with a Philippe Hurel round dining table at its centre and a large Jacques Tati movie poster striking a holiday note. The colour is a mellow tobacco-leaf yellow, developed by Konig with paint specialist Edward Bulmer, who has since added it to his collection with the name 'Trumpington'.[8]

→→ A guest bedroom for children, with patterns on every surface; the bold wallpaper was designed by Nina Campbell.

The kitchen has tall arched windows overlooking the fields behind the house. Here the remains of the medieval deserted village can be discerned (especially in the winter light) in the irregular levels of the landscape. Life revolves around one long oak table, bought from an antique dealer in York especially for the room; fitted around the Aga is a Plain English dresser, designed by Christopher Howe, and painted a dark green. Unusual metal shelves that began life as a French baker's rack were acquired from London dealer-designer William Yeoward. The room is dominated by a vast print of a globe artichoke and striped curtains (in a Lee Jofa fabric).

The south-facing drawing room was also the old entrance hall of the house and has a mellow feel. It is arranged informally but with ample seating, perfect for long conversations in front of a log fire, and there is an especially fine rug acquired from Robert Kime. The green wall colour is also from Bulmer's range, and has the memorable name of Invisible Green. As Konig notes, 'this is the green of Babar the Elephant's coat – a shade that goes with so much as it does in nature'.[9]

This colour, which has the freshness of an English orchard, is an effective foil to a collection of modern British oil paintings and a whole wall dominated by framed Japanese botanical prints of delicate colours. The room is also enhanced by textile covers designed by Nina Campbell, as well as a huge ammonite sculpture, while chairs are a mix of eighteenth- and nineteenth-century antiques and modern pieces.

The playroom at the eastern end of the house has a huge daybed and is hung with signed drawings by the fashion designer Hubert de Givenchy, gifts to Nina Campbell, while the library (which is also the family sitting room) at the south-west corner of the house, has a 1950s-inspired sprig wallpaper from Twigs in Los Angeles, and is hung with watercolours, drawings and prints. A Campbell-designed sofa is covered in a mustard-coloured Tissus d'Hélène corduroy, and instead of a coffee table there is the typical country-house ottoman, both table and seat.

The bedrooms are surprisingly even bolder in their decoration, some with strong-patterned wallpapers and curtains giving them each an individual character; bathrooms have boarded and painted walls. The master bedroom has a handsome four-poster, hung with hand-embroidered lawn curtains that were a gift from Konig's mother and which sit well against a 'pomegranate' wallpaper.

The house has a very personal, comfortable feel, a place for retreat from the bustle of town and city, a house where a writer and a designer and their daughter can enjoy solitude together, which can be filled with friends and family. Even a modestly sized country house can be the repository for a family's treasures and memories. Konig wrote of the North Farm project in late 2019: 'After a year here we felt the house had settled very well and embraced all those that have come to stay. The things that have made it feel like an old soul are the collection of things that we came to the house with, the bed linen, the family pictures and the stuff … It is the stuff which is really the core and soul of a place; it is what completes a house in a way that furniture alone just doesn't'.[10]

→ The Snug Room at Walcot, Oxfordshire, is for listening to music and is decorated with hand-printed fabric from Nathalie Farman-Farma's Décor Barbares.

WALCOT
The modern in the old

OLD HOUSES CAN RESPOND SUR-prisingly well to a modern artistic eye. Walcot in Oxfordshire is the home of the photographer of this volume, Hugo Rittson Thomas, and his wife Silka Rittson Thomas, a renowned art adviser, editor and stylist.[1] Despite its elegant appearance as a small gabled Cotswold stone manor house, it is, surprisingly, only a fragment of a much larger country house that was built in the seventeenth century by the Jenkinson family as their principal seat. The fragment became a tenant farmhouse and was relatively little altered after that period.

This house, of slightly muddled plan but picturesque in form, was, however, in a poor state when Rittson Thomas first saw it, and bought it, in 2001, and he spent several years making it sound and habitable. He remembers, 'some rooms were damp and uninhabitable, but the house did have a kind of energy which I found very compelling and inspired me to take on a rather bigger project than I had first imagined'.[2]

The garden then, he says, 'could only be described as a wilderness – there was nothing, so it was a rather tempting blank canvas to create something fitting and new, so I began looking again for ideas at the gardens I loved most, The Grove, Dean Manor and Hidcote'. But Hugo had grown up in Oxfordshire and had a great fondness for the area, and over the past twenty years he has transformed both house and garden. He and Silka married in 2010, and she has redecorated the interiors with understated style, working collaboratively with close friends such as

→ The gabled Cotswold-stone house now has the charm of a smaller, late sixteenth-century manor house that is the focus of views from a variety of garden compartments.

Christopher Howe, Nathalie Farman-Farma and the upholsterer Lily Wynne Jones.

An estate map dated 1714 was found recently that shows the original substantial Jacobean house of an H-shaped plan with extensive formal gardens to the east and a suite of barns to the west (some of which survive). It was then the seat of Sir Robert Jenkinson, 3rd Baronet, and a Tory MP for Oxfordshire. Sir Robert died in 1717, and the estate passed to his brother (his descendant, Robert Jenkinson, 2nd Earl of Liverpool, was prime minister during the trying times of the Napoleonic Wars). In 1759 the Walcot property was sold to George Spencer, the 4th Duke of Marlborough,[3] who demolished most of the house to provide himself with additional building materials for works on his estate at Blenheim.[4]

The creation of new formal gardens at Walcot was particularly ambitious. They were laid out between 2005 and 2006 with the guidance of designers Julian and Isabel Bannerman, who identified the historic outline of the original house, and introduced balustrades and paths that mark its former footprint and integrate that part of the Walcot narrative into the garden's design. Most importantly, they discovered from antique maps that they located in the Bodleian Library at Oxford the original series of five rectangular mediaeval carp ponds below a spring, thought to have monastic origins. These were the only clues, as their site was then covered by a mature poplar tree wood, so 'a leap of faith was required'.[5]

The ponds step down towards the River Evenlode below. Three of them

↑ Walcot was once a much larger manor house, partly demolished in the mid-eighteenth century when the estate was sold to the Duke of Marlborough; the stones were then used to repair Blenheim's estate walls.

←← The bright and simple double-height dining room has a modern Arts and Crafts flavour. It was formed at the service end of the house in a recent restoration by the removal of a decayed floor.

were excavated by Toti Gifford, the landscape gardener who also runs the famous eponymous Giffords Circus, to create a remarkable shining sculptural element in the wider garden area, one of which is used for swimming. The spoil was formed into a look-out mound in the seventeenth-century manner, on which musical performances have taken place. Landscape gardener Marie-Christine de Laubarède advised on planting over a number of years.

As Polly Devlin observed in *Vogue USA* in 2018, 'the garden incorporates elements of English traditional grand gardening at its best—topiary, allées, pleached lime walks and parterres, meadows, orchards, stone terraces, ancient walls, cascades, and ponds. High, square yew hedges cut like sculpture loom above the swimming-pool garden, where a leprous-looking gargoyle gushes water'.[6]

These elements are used as frames and foils for strong accents of single colour – white flowers in the White Garden, a carpet of red poppies in the old kitchen garden and orchard – but this is also a noticeably green garden, which combined with the warm honey-coloured Cotswold stone walls and terraces, perfectly complements the house and landscape. De Laubarède also advised on the planting of an arboretum.

Silka Rittson Thomas, who is now responsible for new plantings and the design of new gardens, has created a vegetable garden and an orchard carpeted with red poppies and framed by a thyme walk, as well as an organic cutting garden. The latter supplies her London business, The TukTuk Flower Studio in Mayfair. Her mother is a keen gardener, but Silka's childhood home in Germany

was a very different sort of property, a modern glass-walled house in a Japanese spirit.[7] She is committed to connecting art and nature in all aspects of her work.

The White Garden frames Hugo Rittson Thomas's principal modern addition to the house, a large single-volume 'sunken' garden room, a clever take on the timber-framed tradition, under a stone-tile roof. This acts as the main drawing room but almost has the feel of a garden temple or gazebo, with glass walls on two sides.

Both Rittson Thomases are serious collectors and contemporary paintings create a thread of interest and colour throughout the house, while furnishings and textiles have a strong theme of the natural and organic. Objects and fabrics reflect their many travels as well as their friendships with artists and artisans. There is Japanese, Chinese and Mexican earthenware, and Silka also collects Delftware and Japanese vessels for flower arranging. Her collection of ceramics includes works by Judith Hopf, Steven Claydon, Shio Kusaka, Lucie Rie and Hans Coper, and there are paintings by Josef Albers, Rosemarie Trockel, Matt Connors, Isa Genzken and Gillian Carnegie, among others. The art is carefully chosen and displayed and somehow feels very natural against the plain white walls of this thick-walled house.

The overmantel painting in the drawing room is an extraordinary composite piece by Pablo Bronstein that imagines Walcot as a grandiose baroque house before its partial demolition by the 4th Duke of Marlborough. A ceramic bust of a faun-like figure by Claydon faces east along the length of the room, overlooking the long garden axis with the formal pond inspired by David Hicks's black reflection

→ Hugo Rittson Thomas added this new wing to provide a spacious double-height garden-come-drawing room.

A touch of the modern: the great glass doors of this light-filled room can be opened to let in the sights and smells of the elegant semi-formal gardens.

↓ The warm hangings in the Snug Room enhance the acoustics for listening to music.

pond at his Oxfordshire home, The Grove. Furniture is light but textured: there is a Christopher Howe sofa, with cushions from Uzbekistan, and Rose Uniacke fabrics are used in the dining room and main bedroom suite.

The old kitchen has become the dining room and is now open to the roof, like a miniature great hall, with an open fire, stone-flagged floor, whitewashed walls and a scrubbed-oak table. The working kitchen element is inspired by Spanish interiors, and hung with German copper gingerbread moulds and pewter ice cream moulds. The dining room is one of the few rooms still with its late sixteenth-century panelling, and has a memorable Carlo Scarpa chandelier.

The country hats for winter and summer are hung around the boarded 'boot room', which also has a long Gustavian-style timber bench. There is a Snug Room for listening to music decorated with a hand-printed fabric from Silka's close friend Nathalie Farman-Farma's Décor Barbares. Bedrooms are light in colour and themed with faded fabrics and Indian hangings, mostly collected on travels.

The master bedroom suite almost has the feeling of a hut atop a small mountain: bedroom, dressing room and bathroom are all within the former garret spaces of the house. The roof timbers are stripped to their natural colour and waxed, the walls are white, and there are wonderful views over the Oxfordshire landscape.

Hugo Rittson Thomas is a leading portrait photographer, well known for his images of the royal family, and for books on both gardens and architecture. His early career was in film and television. Walcot has been an important home base for him throughout his life as a peripatetic photographer. It is a house of quirky, sculpted gabled stone form and carefully curated artistic gardens. The interiors remain simple and elegant with white walls, natural oak and stone flags, all creating a lovely backdrop for the modern art that the Rittson Thomases love so much.

↙↓ The master bedroom and bathroom suite have been carefully contrived in the original attic spaces of the house.

↑ The dining room with a sixteenth-century fireplace and Carlo Scarpa chandelier.

↑ A detail of the boot room where the walls are hung with hats for all seasons.

← An urn at The Laskett is one of the many classically inspired features that terminate vistas and routes throughout the garden; this one celebrates the Diamond Jubilee of Her Majesty Queen Elizabeth II in 2012.

ENDNOTES

Introduction: On Style

1 James 2009, pp.366–87, and see Cannadine 1990.

2 Girouard 1978, p.300.

3 Goodall 2019, p.9.

4 Seebohm and Sykes 1987, p.39.

5 Gore and Gore 1991, p.9.

6 Girouard 1978, p.318.

7 Pentreath 2016, p.7.

8 Hughes 2005.

9 Ibid., p.66.

10 See especially John Cornforth, Chapter 6, 'John Fowler and the Birth of Humble Elegance', in Cornforth 1985, pp.143–57; and Martin Wood's monographs on Nancy Lancaster and John Fowler (Wood 2005 and Wood 2007 respectively).

11 John Cornforth used this as the subtitle for his *English Interiors: 1790–1848* (1978).

12 Hughes 2005, p.67.

13 Sackville-West 1941, p.40

14 Cornforth 1985, pp.153–54.

Heale House

1 https://www.healegarden.co.uk/gardens (accessed 6 May 2020).

2 Weaver 1915, pp.272–77.

3 Guy and Frances Rasch, interview with the author, 7 September 2019.

4 https://www.healegarden.co.uk/gardens (accessed 6 May 2020).

5 Weaver 1915, p.275.

6 Ibid.

7 Ibid., p.276.

8 Jackson-Stops 1986, p.21.

9 Ibid, p.18 and p.21.

10 Frances Rasch, interview with the author, 14 March 2020.

11 Pownall 2018, pp.70–81.

12 James 1881, vol 1, p.2.

Haddon Hall

1 Cleary 2005; also see Hussey 1949, pp.1651–56, and subsequent articles; and Hall 1996, pp.72–77.

2 James 1905, pp.85–86.

3 Hall 1996, p.72.

4 Ibid.

5 Cecil and Cecil 2012, pp.99–101.

6 D'Abo 2014, p.37.

7 Lady Edward Manners, interview with the author, 14 January 2020.

8 https://www.haddonhall.co.uk/gardens/arne-maynard/ (accessed 6 May 2020).

Beckley Park

1 Lees-Milne 2007, entry for 4 August 1972, p.65.

2 Mowl 2007.

3 Baggs 1996, pp.1–5.

4 Musson 2019, pp.32–47. Some date Beckley Park to c.1540, others to c.1560, but I favour c.1550; Sir John Williams, the likely builder, acquired the park in c.1547 and the manorial title in 1550.

5 Girouard 1978, p.248, and Cooper 1999, pp.113–15.

6 Hussey 1929, p.406.

7 Fitzmaurice 2014, pp.16–25; I am grateful to Laura Fitzmaurice for her advice on Clotilde Brewster's work, from her researches and sharing parts of a new biography now in manuscript.

8 Fitzmaurice 2014, p.17.

9 Ibid., p.22.

10 Quoted in Fitzmaurice 2014, p.23.

11 Hussey 1929, p.408.

12 Clotilde to her brother Christopher, 12 April 1920; The Brewster Archive at San Francesco di Paola, Florence, Italy.

13 Fitzmaurice 2014, p.24.

14 Clotilde to her brother Christopher, 24 December 1919; The Brewster Archive at San Francesco di Paola, Florence, Italy.

15 Huxley 2004, pp.51–52.

16 Percy Feilding to Brewster, 12 December 1920; The Brewster Archive at San Francesco di Paola, Florence, Italy.

17 Countess of Wemyss, interview with the author, 10 October 2019.

18 Lees-Milne 2007, entry for 4 August 1972, p.65.

Lake House

1 Hussey 1937, 27 March, pp.326–31, and 3 April, pp.352–57; and see https://historicengland.org.uk/listing/the-list/list-entry/1001237 (accessed 7 May 2020).

2 Hussey 1937, 27 March, p.327.

3 Ibid., p.354.

4 https://www.architecturaldigest.com/story/sting-trudie-styler-home-wiltshire-england-article (Elizabeth Lambert, January 1996) (accessed 7 May 2020).

5 Styler and Sponzo 1999, p.13.

6 Ibid., p.18.

7 https://www.architecturaldigest.com/story/sting-trudie-styler-home-wiltshire-england-article (Elizabeth Lambert, January 1996) (accessed 7 May 2020).

8 Styler and Sponzo 1999, p.13.

9 Ibid., p.14.

10 Hussey 1937, 27 March, p.327.

Sezincote

1 Head 1982; I am enormously grateful for the valuable researches that Raymond Head has carried out into the story of Sezincote and the evolution of its design – especially Chapter 5.

2 Edward Peake, interview with the author, 16 September 2019, and email communication 28 February 2020.

3 Head 1982, p.83.

4 Firth 2005, p.96.

5 Waugh 1976, p.316.

6 Betjeman 1960, p.99.

7 The S.P. Cockerell designs are held in the RIBA Collections, London, as discussed in detail in Head 1982, pp.39–76.

8 Kingsley 1989, pp.225–28.

9 John Cockerell to his agent Walford, November 1797; https://blogs.ucl.ac.uk/eicah/sezincote-gloucestershire/sezincote-case-study-building-sezincote-building-a-reputation/ (accessed 7 May 2020).

10 Head 1982, p.12.

11 Kingsley 1989, p.225.

12 https://blogs.ucl.ac.uk/eicah/sezincote-gloucestershire/sezincote-case-study-building-sezincote-building-a-reputation/ (accessed 7 May 2020).

13 Thomas Daniell, 'Design for the Indian Bridge at Sezincote, Moreton-in-Marsh', RIBA Collections, RIBA 3951.

14 Conner 1979, p.124.

15 John Claudius Loudon, *Repton's Landscape Gardening*, London 1840, p.367.

16 Heard and Jones 2019, p.143.

17 Kingsley 1989, p.56.

18 Repton's sketch is in the RIBA Collections, London. A copy is in a folder at Sezincote.

19 Head 1982, p.81.

20 Kingsley 1989, p.227.

21 Wood 2007, pp.176–80.

22 Edward Peake, interview with the author, 16 September 2019.

23 Wood 2007, pp.176–77.

24 Ibid.

25 Ibid.

26 The Devoted Classicist.[http://tdclassicist.blogspot.com/2014/07/]

27 http://www.sezincote.co.uk/house-and-garden (accessed 7 May 2020).

On Colour

1 Innes 1981, p.8.

2 Vitruvius 1914, Chapter VII of Book VII.

3 Bristow 1996, p.48.

4 Edward Bulmer, interview with the author, 29 March 2020.

5 Bristow 1996, p.48.

6 Ibid., pp.2–3.

7 See ibid., p.1. Harrison was first published in Raphael Holinshed's *Chronicles of England, Scotlande, and Irelande* in 1577.

8 Bristow 1996, pp.7 and 18–19.

9 Ibid., p.35.

10 Ibid., pp.48–49.

11 Ibid., p.39.

12 Ibid., pp.54–57.

13 Vickery 2009, p.174.

14 Bristow 1996, p.60–66.

15 Baty 2017, p.100, giving the example of work at Newhailes.

16 Saunders 1994, pp.42–55.

17 Bristow 1996, pp.124–28.

18 Ibid., pp.88–92.

19 See ibid., p.99.

20 Ibid., p.161.

21 Ibid., pp.178–79.

22 Baty 2017, p.92.

23 Ibid., pp.64–65.

24 Ibid.; and Bristow 1996, p.203.

25 Bristow 1996, p.201.

26 Baty 2017, p.123.

27 Banham 1994, pp.142–43.

28 Ibid., pp.148–49.

29 Wood 2005, p.36.

30 Wood 2007, p.33.

31 Ibid., p.75.

32 Baty, http://patrickbaty.co.uk/about/ (accessed 6 May 2020).

33 Nina Campbell, interview with the author, 1 April 2020.

34 Rita Konig, interview with the author, 1 April 2020.

35 Edward Bulmer, interview with the author, 1 April 2020.

Vann

1 Haslam 1986, pp.1816–20.

2 Ian MacAlister, revised by Annette Peach, 'Caröe, William Douglas', https://doi.org/10.1093/ref:odnb/32298; Freeman 1990, for Vann, see pp.102–6.

3 Now refurbished as offices for the House of Lords, a project Oliver Caroe worked on.

4 Haslam 1986, p.1818.

5 Lady Adrian, interview with the author, 13 February 2020.

6 Haslam 1986, p.1818.

7 Information from Oliver Caroe, email, 16 February 2020.

8 Brittain-Catlin 2020, p.78.

9 Mary Caroe, interview with the author, 22 February 2020.

10 Ibid.

11 vanngarden.co.uk (accessed 8 May 2020).

12 Ibid.

Smedmore

1 Musson 2015, pp.40–45; and Guilding 2014, pp.114–27.

2 Rowse 2004, p.157.

3 Cecil 1985, p.108.

4 Dr Mansel, interview with the author, 24 September 2019.

5 https://bibleofbritishtaste.com/reminiscences-of-my-visit-to-smedmore (accessed 8 May 2020).

6 Coker 1732, p.46.

7 https://www.historyofparliamenton line.org/volume/1690–1715/member/clavell-edward-1676–1738 (accessed 8 May 2020).

8 Ibid.

9 Musson 2015, pp.42–43.

10 Ibid.

11 Ibid.

12 Ibid.

13 Oswald 1935, pp.62–67.

14 Guilding 2014, p.217.

15 Booton 2015 and https://www.dorsetlife.co.uk/2019/12/dorset-house-smedmore-house/; and information from Dr Mansel.

Beckside House

1 Watkin 1998, pp.149–53; and see Miers 2009, pp.236–40.

2 John Martin Robinson, interview with the author, 2 December 2019.

3 Watkin, 1998, p.152.

4 Ibid.; for the Gibsons of Whelprigg, see Burke 1871, p.500.

5 Robinson 1984.

6 Robinson 2006, p.155.

7 http://patrickbaty.co.uk (accessed 9 May 2020).

8 Powell 1971.

Constable Burton Hall

1 Binney 1968, pp.1396–1401; and Charles Wyvill and D'Arcy and Imogen Wyvill, interviews with the author, 12 September 2019.

2 Colvin 2008, pp.221–29.

3 Ibid., p.221.

4 Ibid., p.225.

5 Wragg 2000, p.2.

6 Hall 2013.

7 For Villa Emo, see *Villa at Emo at Fanzalo, Corpus Palladium*, v, 1970.

8 https://www.architecture.com/image-library/RIBApix/image-information/poster/villa-emo-fanzolo-di-vedelago-plan-and-elevation/posterid/RIBA53460.html (accessed 9 May 2020).

9 Binney 1968, p.1396.

10 D'Arcy and Imogen Wyvill, interviews with the author, 12 September 2019.

11 Britton 1812, XVI, p.722.

12 Information from Charles Wyvill, interview with the author, 12 September 2019.

Pitshill

1 https://www.houseandgarden.co.uk/gallery/pitshill (accessed 9 May 2020); and Charles Pearson, interviews with the author, 7 September 2017 and 25 February 2020.

2 Robinson 2018, pp.50–55; the Grimm drawing is in the British Museum.

3 http://collections.soane.org/THES82362 (accessed 9 May 2020).

4 Musson 2018; also see https://www.houseandgarden.co.uk/gallery/pitshill

5 Ibid., p.107

6 Robinson 2018, pp.50–55.

7 Musson 2018, p.107.

8 Edward Bulmer, interview with the author, 19 February 2020.

9 Musson 2018, p.107.

10 Ibid.

11 Robinson 2018, pp.50–51.

Chyknell Hall

1 Princess Corinna zu Sayn-Wittgenstein-Sayn, interview with the author, 13 December 2019.

2 Tollemache 2020; I am grateful for access to the draft of this excellent research document.

3 Tollemache 2020, p.12.

4 Ibid., pp.14–15.

5 Ibid., 2020, p.12.

6 Ibid., p.20.

7 Princess Corinna zu Sayn-Wittgenstein-Sayn, interview with the author, 13 December 2019.

8 Guy Goodfellow, interview with the author, 9 January 2020.

9 Princess Corinna zu Sayn-Wittgenstein-Sayn, interview with the author, 13 December 2019.

10 Guy Goodfellow, interview with the author, 9 January 2020.

On Furniture

1 Musson 2005, pp.208–19.

2 See Simon Swynfen Jervis, 'Furniture at Hardwick Hall – I', in Adshead 2016, pp.87–109.

3 Irving 1819, p.90 (quoted from the revised edition, 1848).

4 Musson 2005, p.209; Harrison's account first appears in Holinshed 1577.

5 Clive Edwards in 'The Beginning of the Present: Stability and Professionalism', Edwards 2010, pp.3–7, esp. pp.4–5.

6 Clive Edwards, 'The Seventeenth Century: Architects and Activists', in Edwards 2010, pp.13–20.

7 Ibid., p.14

8 Ibid., pp.14–15.

9 Ibid., p.15.

10 Musson 2009, p.225.

11 Treve Rosoman, 'The Eighteenth Century: Inspiration and Individualism', in Edwards 2010, pp.33–39.

12 Chippendale 1754, preface.

13 Quoted in Edwards 2010, p.38.

14 Musson 1999, pp.215–16.

15 Ibid.

16 Ibid., p.218; and also see Jonathan Meyer, 'The Nineteenth Century: Empire and Eclecticism', pp.109–12, in Edwards 2010, and Michael Barrington, 'The Arts and Crafts Movement: Origins and Ideals', pp.189–97, in Edwards 2010.

17 Musson 1999, p.19; see the photograph of the interior of Great Dixter.

18 https://www.nytimes.com/1993/06/13/books/sweet-ottoline.html

19 Shapland 1909, p.5.

20 Musson 1999, pp.117–18.

21 Ibid., pp.111–14.

22 Seebohm and Sykes 1987, p.viii.

23 For John Fowler's influential career see Wood 2007.

24 Mlinaric and Cecil 2008, pp.10–11.

25 Ibid., pp.11–12.

Wolverton Hall

1 Nicholas and Georgia Coleridge, interview with the author, 19 August 2019.

2 For the work of Quinlan Terry generally, see Watkin 2006.

3 Nicholas and Georgia Coleridge, interview with the author, 19 August, 2019.

4 Ibid.

5 https://landedfamilies.blogspot.com/2013/03/20-acton-of-lower-wolverton-hall.html (accessed 9 May 2020).

6 Brooks and Pevsner 2007, pp.521, 610.

7 I am grateful to Dr Simon Thurley for this observation.

8 https://landedfamilies.blogspot.com/2013/03/20-acton-of-lower-wolverton-hall.html (accessed 9 May 2020).

9 Information from Georgia Coleridge, email to the author, 13 March 2020.

10 Nicholas and Georgia Coleridge, interview with the author, 19 August, 2019.

11 Tyzack 2012.

12 Lowry and Wilks 2002.

13 https://www.coleshillhouse.com/worcestershire-group-leaders-and-the-van-moppes.php (accessed 9 May 2020).

Eastridge

1 Site visit 26 September 2019.

2 Francis Terry is chairman of TAG, the traditional architects group of RIBA-qualified architects, and was recognised in the exhibition *Three Classicists* at RIBA in 2010; see the accompanying book by Dan Cruickshank.

3 Francis Terry, interview with the author, 26 September, 2019.

4 Messel 2011, especially Jeremy Musson, Chapter 5, 'Messel as Interpreter of the Caribbean Palladian Style', pp.144–223.

5 http://www.jrdesign.org/about (accessed 11 May 2020).

6 Musson 2006, pp.76–81.

7 Watkin 2006, pp.152–63.

8 Watkin 2015, pp.16–19.

9 Ibid., pp.28–71, and for Ferne Park, pp.71–88; and see Watkin 2006, pp.206–71.

Court of Noke

1 Robinson 2010, pp.63–67.

2 Ibid., p.63.

3 Ibid.

4 Edward and Emma Bulmer, interviews with the author, 6 August 2019.

5 Mlinaric and Cecil 2008.

6 Edward and Emma Bulmer, interviews with the author, 6 August 2019.

7 Ibid.

8 Robinson 2010, p.64.

9 Ibid.

10 https://collection.sciencemuseumgroup.org.uk/people/cp132912/cherry-kearton (accessed 11 May 2020).

11 https://www.countrylife.co.uk/interiors/antique-wallpaper-extraordinary-edward-bulmer-built-entire-room-around-even-raised-ceiling-195419 (accessed 7 May 2020).

Voewood

1 https://historicengland.org.uk/listing/the-list/list-entry/1001428; and Pevsner and Wilson 1999.

2 Simon Finch, interview with the author, 4 November 2019.

3 Cook 2015, pp.92–101.

4 Cruickshank 1999, p.8.

5 The original designs are in a private collection in Norfolk.

6 Weaver 1909, p.640.

7 Ibid., p.637.

8 Ibid.

9 Cook 2015, pp.70–79.

10 Morris 2004.

The Laskett

1 See Strong 2017, which is the most recent edition of a compilation of these columns.

2 Sir Roy Strong CH, interview with the author, 23 July 2019.

3 Strong 2017, p.13.

4 Ibid.

5 Musson 2010, pp.54–59.

6 Sir Roy Strong CH, interview with the author, 23 July 2019 (the late John Cornforth was the architectural editor of *Country Life* from 1967 to 1977).

7 Ibid.

8 Draft of diary by kind permission.

9 Sir Roy Strong CH, interview with the author, 23 July 2019.

10 Strong 2017, p.18.

11 Ibid.

12 Ibid.

13 Strong 2017, p.19.

14 Ibid.

On Gardens

1 Richardson 2009, p.379.

2 Jellicoe and Jellicoe 1991, p.165.

3 Gillat-Ray 2010, pp.17–18.

4 Jellicoe and Jellicoe 1991, p.164.

5 Ibid., p.165.

6 Muthesius 2007, vol. I, p.212.

7 Richardson 2009, p.380.

8 Dixon Hunt and Willis 1988, p.124.

9 Jellicoe and Jellicoe 1991, p.167.

10 Ibid.

11 Dixon Hunt 2012, p.178.

12 Jellicoe and Jellicoe 1991, p.167.

13 Richardson 2009, p.383.

14 Ibid., p.383.

15 Turner 1985, pp.163–164.

16 Richardson 2009, p.382.

17 Ibid., p.383.

18 Muthesius 2007, vol. I, p.219.

19 Richardson 2009, p.383.

20 Horwood 2010, p.126.

21 Page, https://www.greatbritishgardens.co.uk/russell-page.html (accessed 4 May 2020).

22 Evelyn 1669, introduction.

Draycot House

1 https://www.british-history.ac.uk/vch/wilts/vol9/pp43–49 (accessed 11 May 2020).

2 Site visit 18 November 2019.

3 Emily Todhunter, interview with the author, 18 November 2019.

4 Ibid.

5 Hillier 2007, pp.248–49, 262–63.

6 Emily Todhunter, interview with the author, 18 November 2019.

7 Ibid.

8 http://www.todhunterearle.com/wp-content/uploads/2019/06/Introspective-Mag-Jun-2019-TEI-Profile.pdf (accessed 12 May 2020).

9 For the private apartments at Sissinghurst as occupied by Nigel Nicolson, see Musson 2002, pp.132–35.

10 Emily Todhunter, interview with the author, 18 November 2019.

11 Ibid.

12 Merton 2003.

13 Emily Todhunter, interview with the author, 18 November 2019.

Ham Court

1 https://www.british-history.ac.uk/vch/oxon/vol13/pp22–30#anchorn44; and Brooks and Sherwood 2017, pp.105–6.

2 Site visit and interview with Matthew Rice, 7 May 2020.

3 https://www.bloomsbury.com/uk/search?q=matthew+rice&Gid=1

4 For Aymer de Valence, see Phillips 1972.

5 Dr Nick Doggett, 'Statement of Significance: Ham Court Bampton – Phase I – the Long Barn', April 2011.

6 Brooks and Sherwood 2017, p.105.

7 Matthew Rice, interview with the author, 7 May 2019.

8 https://www.british-history.ac.uk/vch/oxon/vol13/pp22–30#anchorn44

9 https://www.gardensillustrated.com/gardens/country/garden-moated-gatehouse-emma-bridgewater/ (Non Morris, January 9, 2020).

10 Matthew Rice, interview with the author, 7 May 2019.

11 Ibid.

North Farm

1 https://britishlistedbuildings.co.uk/101323001-barn-to-north-of-north-farm-farmhouse-walworth (accessed 12 May 2020).

2 Letter on the history of the Walworth estate and Eade family from Philip Eade, 8 December 2019.

3 https://www.rlf.org.uk/fellowships/philip-eade/ (accessed 12 May 2020).

4 *The Northern Echo*, 9 September 2018.

5 https://ritakonig.com (accessed 12 May 2020); site visit and interview with Rita Konig, 28 October 2019.

6 Ibid.

7 Ibid.

8 https://ritakonig.com (accessed 12 May 2020).

9 Rita Konig, interview with author, 28 October 2019.

10 Rita Konig, draft of a piece written for *House and Garden*, shared with the author, 27 November 2019.

Walcot

1 Summerly 2017, pp.131–34.

2 Hugo Rittson Thomas, interview with the author, 12 March 2020.

3 For the sale and extent of the Marlborough estates in Charlbury parish, see https://www.british-history.ac.uk/vch/oxon/vol10/pp127–157 (accessed 12 May 2020).

4 Hugo Rittson Thomas, interview with the author, 12 March 2020.

5 Ibid.

6 Devlin 2018, p.112.

7 Silka Rittson Thomas, interview with the author, 18 February 2020.

SELECT BIBLIOGRAPHY

DAVID ADSHEAD AND DAVID A.H.B. TAYLOR (EDS), *Hardwick Hall: A Great Old Castle of Romance*, London and New Haven, 2016

A.P. BAGGS, ET AL, 'Bampton Hundred', in *A History of the County of Oxford: Volume 13, Bampton Hundred (Part I)*, eds. Alan Crossley and C.R.J. Currie (London, 1996), pp.1–5

JOANNA BANHAM, 1994, 'The English Response: Mechanization and Design Reform', in Hoskins 1994, pp.132–149

PATRICK BATY, 2017, *The Anatomy of Colour: The Story of Heritage Paints and Pigments*, London: Thames & Hudson

JOHN BETJEMAN, 1960, *Summoned by Bells*, London: John Murray

MARCUS BINNEY, 28 November 1968, 'Constable Burton Hall, Yorkshire', *Country Life*, pp.1396–1401

PETER BOOTON, March 2015, 'Behind the Scenes Look at Smedmore House, Purbeck', *Dorset Magazine*; https://www.dorsetmagazine.co.uk/out-about/places/behind-the-scenes-look-at-smedmore-estate-in-purbeck-1-3992510

IAN BRISTOW, 1996, *Architectural Colour in British Interiors: 1615–1840*, New Haven and London: Yale University Press

TIMOTHY BRITTAIN-CATLIN, 2020, *The Edwardians and Their Houses: The New Life of Old England*, London: Lund Humphries

JOHN BRITTON, 1812, *The Beauties of England and Wales*, vol VI, London: Vernor & Hood

ALAN BROOKS AND NIKOLAUS PEVSNER, 2007, *The Buildings of England: Worcestershire*, 2nd ed, New Haven and London: Yale University Press

ALAN BROOKS AND JENNIFER SHERWOOD, 2017, *The Buildings of England: Oxfordshire North and West*, New Haven and London: Yale University Press

BERNARD BURKE, 1871, *A Genealogical and Heraldic History of the Landed Gentry of Great Britain & Ireland*, London: Harrison

DAVID CANNADINE, 1990, *The Decline and Fall of the British Aristocracy*, New Haven and London: Yale University Press

LORD DAVID CECIL, 1985, *Some Dorset Country Houses*, Wimborne: The Dovecote Press

HUGH AND MIRABEL CECIL, 2012, *In Search of Rex Whistler: His Life and His Work*, London: Pimpernel Press

THOMAS CHIPPENDALE, 1754, *The Gentleman and Cabinet-Maker's Director*, London: printed by the author

BRYAN CLEARY, 2005, *Haddon Hall, Bakewell, Derbyshire: The Home of Lord Edward Manners*, Derby: Heritage House Group Ltd

JOHN COKER, 1732, *A Survey of Dorsetshire: Containing the Antiquities and Natural History of That County … And a Copious Genealogical Account of Three Hundred of the Principal Families*, London: printed for J. Wilcox

HOWARD COLVIN, 2008, *A Biographical Dictionary of British Architects: 1600–1840*, New Haven and London: Yale University Press

PATRICK CONNER, 1979, *Oriental Architecture in the West*, London: Thames & Hudson

MARTIN COOK, 2015, *Edward Prior: Arts and Crafts Architect*, Ramsbury: The Crowood Press

NICHOLAS COOPER, 1999, *Houses of Gentry, 1480–1680*, New Haven and London: Yale University Press

JOHN CORNFORTH, 1985, *The Inspiration of the Past: Country House Taste in the Twentieth Century*, London: Viking

DAN CRUICKSHANK, 18 November 1999, 'Material Values: E.S. Prior's Home Place, Norfolk', *Architectural Journal*, pp.46–49

DAN CRUICKSHANK, 2010, *Three Classicists*, London: RIBA Publications, 2010

LADY URSULA D'ABO, 2014, *The Girl with the Widow's Peak: The Memoirs*, ed. David Watkin, London: d'Abo Publications

POLLY DEVLIN, June 2018, 'The Secret Garden', *Vogue USA*, pp.108–15

JOHN DIXON HUNT AND PETER WILLIS (EDS), 1988, *The Genius of the Place: The English Landscape Garden 1620–1820*, Cambridge, MA: MIT Press

JOHN DIXON HUNT, 2012, *A World of Gardens: The English Landscape 1620–1820*, London: Reaktion Books

CLIVE EDWARDS ET AL, 2010, *British Furniture 1600–2000*, Wimbledon: The Intelligent Layman

JOHN EVELYN, 1669, *Kalendarium Hortense*, London: Printed by Jo. Martyn and Ja. Allestry

ALLEN FIRTH, 2005, *The Book of Bourton-on-the-Hill, Batsford and Sezincote*, Tiverton: Halsgrave

LAURA FITZMAURICE, Fall 2014, 'Clotilde Brewster: American Expatriate Architect', *Nineteenth Century, the Magazine of the Victorian Society in America*, vol.34, no.2, pp.16–25

JENNIFER FREEMAN, 1990, *W.D. Caröe: His Architectural Achievement*, Manchester: Manchester University Press

SOPHIE GILLIAT-RAY, 2010, *Islamic Gardens in the UK*, London: Calouste Gulbenkian Foundation

MARK GIROUARD, 1978, *Life in the English Country House*, New Haven and London: Yale University Press

JOHN GOODALL, 2019, *English House Style: From the Archives of* Country Life, New York: Rizzoli International Publications

ALAN AND ANNE GORE, 1991, *The History of English Interior Decoration*, London: Phaidon

RUTH GUILDING, July 2014, 'Estate Expectations', *World of Interiors*, pp.114–27

MICHAEL HALL, 27 June 1996, 'Haddon Hall, Derbyshire', *Country Life*, pp.72–77

IVAN HALL, 2013, *John Carr of York: A Pictorial Survey*, Horbury: Rickaro Books Ltd

RICHARD HASLAM, 26 June 1986, 'Vann, Surrey', *Country Life*, pp.1816–20

RAYMOND HEAD, 1982, 'Sezincote: A Paradigm', MA thesis, Royal College of Art, London

KATE HEARD AND KATHRYN JONES, 2019, *George IV: Art & Spectacle*, London: Royal Collection Trust

BEVIS HILLIER, 2007, *John Betjeman: The Biography*, London: John Murray

RAPHAEL HOLINSHED, 1577, *Chronicles of England, Scotlande, and Irelande*, London: imprinted for George Bishop

CATHERINE HORWOOD, 2010, *Gardening Women*, London: Virago

LESLEY HOSKINS (ED.), 1994, *The Papered Wall, The History, Patterns and Techniques of Wallpaper*, London: Thames & Hudson

HELEN HUGHES (ED.), 2005, *John Fowler: The Invention of Country-House Style*, London: Routledge

CHRISTOPHER HUSSEY, 3 March 1929, 'Beckley Park, Oxfordshire', *Country Life*, pp.400–8

CHRISTOPHER HUSSEY, 1937, 'Lake House I and II', *Country Life*, 27 March, pp.326–31; 3 April, pp.352–57

CHRISTOPHER HUSSEY, 22 December 1949, 'Haddon Hall, Derbyshire – I', *Country Life*, pp.1651–56 (and five consecutive weeks)

ALDOUS HUXLEY, 2004, *Crome Yellow*, London: Vintage Classics

JOCASTA INNES, 1981, *Paint Magic*, London: Frances Lincoln

WASHINGTON IRVING, 1819, *The Sketchbook of Geoffrey Crayon Gent.*, New York: G.P. Putnam & Co.

GERVASE JACKSON-STOPS, 3 July 1986, 'From Craft to Art', *Country Life*, pp.18–22

HENRY JAMES, 1881, *The Portrait of a Lady*, vol 1, London: Macmillan & Co

Henry James, 1905, *English Hours*, Cambridge, ma: Riverside Press

Lawrence James, 2009, *Aristocrats*, London: Little, Brown & Company

Geoffrey and Susan Jellicoe (eds), 1991, *The Oxford Companions to Gardens*, Oxford: Oxford University Press

Nicholas Kingsley, 1989, *The Country Houses of Gloucestershire*, vol ii, *1660–1830*, Bognor Regis: Phillimore & Co. Ltd

James Lees-Milne, 2007, *Diaries 1971–1983*, London: John Murray

Bernard Lowry and Mick Wilks, 2002, *The Mercian Maquis, the Secret Resistance Organisation in Herefordshire and Worcestershire During World War ii*, Eardisley: Logaston Press

John Merton, 2003, *Journey Through an Artist's Life*, Turin: Umberto Allemandi

Thomas Messel (ed), 2011, *Oliver Messel: In the Theatre of Design*, New York: Rizzoli International

Mary Miers, 2009, *The English Country House*, New York: Rizzoli International Publications

Mary Miers, 25 February 2009, 'Butterfly Dream: Voewood, Norfolk', *Country Life*, pp.38–43

David Mlinaric and Mirabel Cecil, 2008, *Mlinaric on Decorating*, New York: Prestel

Belinda Morris, 24 September 2004, 'Manor from Heaven', *The Observer*

Timothy Mowl, 2007, *The Historic Gardens of England: Oxfordshire*, Stroud: Tempus Publishing

Jeremy Musson, 1999, *The English Manor House*, London: Aurum

Jeremy Musson, 5 September 2002, 'Sissinghurst Castle, Kent', *Country Life*, pp.132–35

Jeremy Musson, 2005, *How to Read a Country House*, London: Ebury

Jeremy Musson, 'Chilham Castle, Kent ii', *Country Life*, 13 July 2006, pp.76–81

Jeremy Musson, 2009, 'The English Country House and Its Collections', in Miers 2009, pp.225–27

Jeremy Musson, 1 September 2010, 'Awake the Muse: The Laskett', *Country Life*, pp.54–59

Jeremy Musson, 4 February 2015, 'A Dream of a Place: Smedmore House', *Country Life*, pp.40–45

Jeremy Musson, 'A neo-classical idyll', *House and Garden*, November 2018, pp.106–115

Jeremy Musson, 2019, *Rycote*, Peterborough: Jarrold

Hermann Muthesius, 2007, *The English House* (1904–5), translated from the German by Dennis Sharp, 2 vols, London: Frances Lincoln

Arthur Oswald, 19 January 1935, 'Smedmore, Dorset', *Country Life*, pp.62–67

Ben Pentreath, 2012, *English Decoration*, London and New York: Ryland Peter & Small

Ben Pentreath, 2016, *English Houses*, London and New York: Ryland Peters & Small

Nikolaus Pevsner and James Bettley, 2015, *Buildings of England: Suffolk*, New Haven and London: Yale University Press

Nikolaus Pevsner and Bill Wilson, 1999, *Buildings of England: Norfolk 2: North-West and South*, New Haven and London: Yale University Press

John Roland Seymour Phillips, 1972, *Aymer de Valence: Earl of Pembroke 1307–1324. Baronial Politics in the Reign of Edward ii*, Oxford: Clarendon Press

Anthony Powell, 1971, *Books Do Furnish a Room*, London: Little, Brown and Company

Elfreda Pownall, September 2018, 'Good for the Souls', *World of Interiors*, pp.78–81

Tim Richardson, 2009, 'The Landscapes and Gardens of the English Country House', in Miers 2009, pp.379–84

John Martin Robinson, 1984, *The Latest Country Houses*, London: Constable

John Martin Robinson, 2006, *Grass Seed in June*, Wilby: Michael Russell Publishing Ltd

John Martin Robinson, 20 October 2010, 'An English Fairy Tale: The Court of Noke', *Country Life*, pp.63–67

John Martin Robinson, 21 November 2018, 'Back to the Future', *Country Life*, pp.50–55

Alfred Leslie Rowse, 2004, *The Diaries of A.L. Rowse*, ed. Richard Ollard, London: Penguin

Vita Sackville-West, 1941, *English Country Houses*, London: William Collins

Gill Saunders, 1994, 'The China Trade: Oriental Painted Panels', pp.42–55, in Hoskins 1994

Caroline Seebohm and Christopher Simon Sykes, 1987, *English Country: Living in England's Private Houses*, London: Thames & Hudson

Henry Shapland, 1909, *Style Schemes in Antique Furnishing*, London: Simpkin, Marshall, Hamilton, Kent, Benn

Roy Strong, 2017, *A Country Life: At Home in the English Countryside*, Hereford: Impact

Trudie Styler and Joseph Sponzo, 1999, *The Lake House Cookbook*, New York and London: Clarkson Potter

Victoria Summerly, 2017, *Secret Houses of the Cotswolds*, London: Frances Lincoln

Michael Tollemache, 2020, *The Book of Chyknell*, manuscript to be published (at press time)

Roger Turner, 1985, *Capability Brown and the Eighteenth Century English Landscape*, London: Weidenfeld & Nicolson

Anna Tyzack, 7 November 2012, 'My Perfect Weekend: Nicholas Coleridge', *Daily Telegraph*

Amanda Vickery, 2009, *Behind Closed Doors: At Home in Georgian England*, New Haven and London: Yale University Press

Vitruvius, 1914, *The Ten Books on Architecture*, ed. Morris Hicky Morgan, Oxford: Oxford University Press

David Watkin, 10 September 1998, 'Beckside House', *Country Life*, pp.148–53

David Watkin, 2006, *Radical Classicism: The Architecture of Quinlan Terry*, London: Random House Incorporated

David Watkin, 2015, *Practice of Classical Architecture: The Architecture of Quinlan and Francis Terry, 2005–15*, New York: Rizzoli International Publications

Evelyn Waugh, 1976, *The Diaries of Evelyn Waugh*, ed. Michael Davie, London: Weidenfeld & Nicolson

Lawrence Weaver, 6 November 1909, 'Home Place, Holt', *Country Life*, pp.634–642

Lawrence Weaver, 1915, 'Heale House, Wiltshire i and ii', *Country Life*, March 27, pp.326–332; April 3, pp.352–357

Anthony Wells-Cole, 1994, 'Flocks, Florals, and Fancies: English Manufacture 1680–1830', pp.22–41, in Hoskins 1994

Martin Wood, 2005, *Nancy Lancaster: English Country House Style*, London: Frances Lincoln

Martin Wood, 2007, *John Fowler: Prince of Decorators*, London: Frances Lincoln

Brian Wragg, 2000, *John Carr of York*, ed. Giles Worsley, York: Oblong Creative

Arabella Youens, 19 April 2019, 'Home and Interiors', *Country Life*; https://www.countrylife.co.uk/interiors/antique-wallpaper-extraordinary-edward-bulmer-built-entire-room-around-even-raised-ceiling-195419

INDEX

ACKNOWLEDGEMENTS

My first and warmest thanks are to all the owners and occupants of the delectable houses included in this volume, for their generosity in allowing us to include their homes in such a book, and for what they all do to keep fine houses together and lived in and cherished; thanks too for their hospitality, kindness and company on our visits, and especially for their efforts to help me better understand their houses. All the visits were done before the 2020 pandemic, and some of those whose homes are featured suffered from the virus. Sadly, Mary Caroe, died from the virus, which is such a great loss to us all, but I am pleased that the house and garden are here recorded as she knew and loved them. For me, such times only reinforce the cultural and spiritual importance of the historic houses and gardens in our midst. They not only are potent symbols of survival, continuity and peaceful retreat, they also give to all of us, beyond the families who own them and live in them, great pleasure and inspiration.

Rizzoli produces the most beautiful books, and it is always a privilege to be asked to help put one together. Special thanks to Rizzoli publisher Charles Miers for inviting myself and Hugo Rittson Thomas to do the book and for his continued enthusiasm and support; to Hugo Rittson Thomas for his wonderful photographs, support and patience during this project; to Andrea Danese who has been a very supportive editor, taking a great interest in it from the start; and to Robert Dalrymple, once again, for his superlative and enticing design.

Many others have helped, including Linda Schofield with valuable copyediting, Senga Fairgrieve with typesetting and Marian Appellof with proofreading; Helena Bradbury and Jasmin Barrowclough from Hugo's studio on arrangements for visits and follow up; and Neil Parker, Helen Bradbury and Hannah Kirkham who support me in so much of my work. Others who have given useful input from reading my texts or advising on content to giving me support as a writer include Timothy Brittain-Catlin, Edward Bulmer, Nina Campbell, Oliver Caroe, Ptolemy Dean, Leslie Geddes-Brown, John Goodall, Guy Goodfellow, Julian Litten, Mary Miers, Will Palin, Tim Richardson, Harriet Salisbury, Michael Tollemache and Christopher Woodward. As always I am grateful to the librarians of the London Library and the University of Cambridge for their help in sourcing the books necessary to write other books, and to those authors who are naturally acknowledged throughout in the notes and bibliography.

And to my wife Sophie, and daughters Georgia and Miranda, thanks as always for their patience, support and love – and to Archie the Jack Russell, a constant companion when I am at the desk writing.
JEREMY MUSSON

My sincere and heartfelt thanks to each homeowner for their generosity of time and incredible patience, and who have shared their homes with such enthusiasm. I have thoroughly enjoyed photographing every home.

I would like to echo Jeremy's praise for Rizzoli, and give a special thanks to Charles Miers and Andrea Danese who have guided this book to its final form with the greatest of care and insight. A special thanks also goes to Robert Dalrymple for his forbearance and wonderful eye.

It is always a pleasure to work with Jeremy, and a great thank you to him for his impressive and engaging text. My darling wife Silka, thank you for your help and support during the long days, and for your valued input on everything I do. In my studio Helena Bradbury has been a valuable asset, and thank you also to Henry Hunt.
HUGO RITTSON THOMAS

To Lucy Lambton, architectural enthusiast, inspirational author and friend. JM

First published in the United States of American in 2021
By Rizzoli International Publications, Inc.
300 Park Avenue South · New York, NY 10010

www.rizzoliusa.com

Text copyright © 2021 by Jeremy Musson
Photographs © 2021 by Hugo Rittson Thomas

Publisher: Charles Miers
Editor: Andrea Danese
Design: Robert Dalrymple
Production Manager: Kaija Markoe

Printed in Hong Kong

2021 2022 2023 2024 / 10 9 8 7 6 5 4 3 2 1

ISBN: 978-0-8478-6985-5

Library of Congress Control Number: 2020945412

Visit us online:
Facebook.com/RizzoliNewYork
Twitter: @Rizzoli_Books
Instagram.com/RizzoliBooks
Pinterest.com/RizzoliBooks
Youtube.com/user/RizzoliNY
Issuu.com/Rizzoli

Of the houses featured in this book, only Haddon Hall and Sezincote are open to the public on occasion. Their gardens and those of Heale House, The Laskett and Vann are also open for visits on occasion. For visitor information, please consult the house websites.

→ Endpapers: Jasmine Dot from the Paradise Restored collection, Hamilton Weston Wallpapers.